Junior Assemblies

edited by Geraldine Witcher

illustrations by Elizabeth Norman-Clarke

Scripture Union

130 City Road, London EC1V 2NJ

List of contributors

Mr Bentley (5,8)
Mrs Boydell (6,7,35)
Mr Brittain (19)
Miss S. Eccles (11,16)
Mr Edwards (9)
Mrs Jessiman (25)
Miss S. Montgomery (30,37)
Miss C. Morgan (14)
Mr Moulson (38)
Miss M. Ralph (22,23,27,29)
Mr Rawlings (2,3,13,15,24,28,33,36)
Mrs Siggars (1,18)
Mrs J. Simmonds (21)
Mrs G. Witcher (4,17,26,32,34)
Mrs Wright (10,12,25,31,39)

© Scripture Union 1982
Reprinted 1985, 1986, 1989, 1990

ISBN 0 85421 949 8

Printed and bound in Great Britain by
Ebenezer Baylis & Son Limited,
The Trinity Press, Worcester, and London

CONTENTS

Making full use of the book

'Whatever am I going to do with my class for our assembly?' – a question that most teachers have to find an answer to at some stage during the school year. This book aims to provide answers to that question. It contains thirty-nine assembly outlines – one for each week of the school year, for use with a class of junior age children. All are written so that they will involve the whole class in some capacity, giving opportunity for participation in varying ways: singing, making music, acting, drawing and painting, reading and so on. They are offered as suggestions for teachers to adapt to suit their own situation. Some may want to have their pupils write their own drama, for example.

Each outline includes a Bible base section, intended as background preparation for the teacher and not intended to be read by the children.

The outlines all draw on biblical material, in a way that makes the Bible story both clear and relevant to children today. There are four sections to choose from: Old Testament, Life of Jesus and Early Church, Stories Jesus Told, and Special Occasions (which in addition to the usual Christmas, Easter and Harvest suggestions contains ideas for a Sports Day assembly, and a Leavers Farewell among others!). There is also a simple cross-reference system so that the teacher can see other outlines on related topics.

Each outline contains suggestions for preparation work in class with the children who are to give the assembly and also follow-up work which may be used both with those who 'performed' and those who watched. It is hoped that in this way the assembly will be seen as part of the ongoing work of the class and not just a special, and perhaps irrelevant activity. To help with class work there is a resources section at the end of the book.

Looking through the book you will notice that there is a wide range of content, style and complexity in the outlines. It is hoped that this will ensure that there is something within the scope of the youngest children, and the most inexperienced teacher, as well as something to challenge the older classes. There is also a section giving hints on various aspects of the outlines, using choral speaking with children, for example, or how to adapt to a specific situation.

It is suggested that you use the Good News version of the Bible in any work you do with the children, and this is the version that has generally been quoted throughout this book. There are children's versions of this Bible available.

Finally, it is hoped that this book will provide new ideas for those who already use the Bible in assembly, and inspire those who have been reluctant to use it.

Music in assembly

Music is an essential part of an assembly in most schools. Whether it is singing a favourite song, expressing praise and worship through the singing of a hymn, listening to a tape or record of great classical music, or the performance by children of original or learned pieces, music has a way of bringing the whole school together. The shared act of listening or participation creates a bond between the children.

Music can be used to bring the children together, then, at the beginning or end of an assembly, or at strategic points throughout. It can also be used to create a mood. When the children come in all excited, because it is very windy, or the first snowfall of the year, a few minutes listening to quiet music will make them more ready to listen and respond. Music can be used to 'set the scene' for the rest of the assembly; martial music for a battle, wild music for a storm at sea, and so on.

Music can be added in many places in these assembly outlines. Often it is suggested, but background music can be played in many other places, and it can intersperse narrative when the actors need extra time.

Hymns have been suggested in these outlines. You will of course have your own particular repertory of hymns and songs, which you may wish to use instead. Singing hymns that everyone knows is a good way of including all the children in the hall in the assembly. But for a change, why not let the 'performing' class sing a new song, and then teach it to the rest of the school. It may then become a favourite!

Music, whether it be singing, listening or performing, should be fun. The children should be encouraged to experiment with percussion instruments for sound effects, and to use their ideas in assemblies. If you have any children with particular talents, such as playing the piano or guitar, these can be included in your assembly. It might make a nice change for the pianist to sit back and listen to guitars accompanying the singing.

If you wish to tape music for playing in assembly, make sure the amplification is adequate. In a small hall this is a good way of getting over the problem of the insufficient children to do all that is required, but taped music can sound dreadful, or not be heard at all, in large rooms.

If there is no pianist, and children are unable to accompany hymns, they can either be sung unaccompanied, perhaps with rhythmic hand clapping, or you could use a tape or record. This again is an opportunity for learning new songs.

The more the children can take over the music side of an assembly the better; it is another medium of communication open to them, and will encourage a lively interested attitude towards music of all kinds.

Children as actors

Children are natural actors; much of their play is in the form of pretending to be something or someone they are not. They spend hours in a world of their own, which is often more real to them than the world we adults live in! So when we are asking them to act in school, we are merely extending this natural instinct and giving direction and limits to it. When children participate in drama, the story and characters become far more real to them than if they just read the story. Similarly watching a play is a more vivid experience than listening to a story.

Drama has been a vehicle for teaching religious truths for centuries; this method was used in the Mystery plays of the Middle Ages. Dance and dramatic presentation are part of other religions too. We are carrying on this tradition, when we ask our children to act for assembly.

Having said all this, we have to admit that there are children who really have no idea of what to do or say when on stage. There should be minor parts for these, or some other important task, and lots of encouragement to join in.

While presenting an assembly should be enjoyable for both children and teacher, it is work, and so we should expect a reasonable standard of performance. We should try to get a polished performance which will satisfy the performers and entertain the watchers. This means you should not let rehearsals become giggly, or there is the danger that the giggles will recur during the assembly!

Learning words for a play is not such a hard task as we often think. Children usually learn quickly, and the chance to be in the play is an encouragement here. Remember to tell the children to face the audience when they are speaking, and to address their words to the back of the hall, but without shouting. Listen to the play during rehearsal from the back to make sure the words are carrying.

Props and costumes need not be elaborate; much of the scenery in these outlines consists of a sheet of corrugated card representing walls, buildings etc. For costumes, a lot can be done with a few sheets of material to drape or tie.

Discussion of how a rehearsal went, what should be changed, how a certain point can be made more alive, are all valid parts of a drama session. The play will be that much better if suggestions come from the children.

Finally, these plays are given as suggestions to be adapted to suit your class, your school, your abilities. If it *sounds* wrong when your children say it, then it *is* wrong. Words can be altered, put into dialect if you like, until the result is yours and the child's, and right for your particular situation. And as a final point to the children, tell them that acting is fun!

Choral speaking

One very effective method of preparing passages of prose or poems for performance in an assembly is to use choral speech. This is a form of delivery by several groups of children, using a variety of numbers and voice qualities to maintain interest in what is being spoken. It has the advantage of audibility; as many voices as necessary can be used, and children are less inhibited when speaking with others than they would be when asked to read or recite alone. Long passages are broken up into parts, with each section being read by a different combination of children. Variations in speed and volume also increase the interest. Stage blocks, benches, chairs, stools can all be used to make an interesting grouping on various levels and there is no reason why solo voices cannot be used. An added virtue of presenting a piece in this way is that a capable but nervous child is encouraged to participate and a lively, outgoing child is contained without the need to 'squash' him too forcibly.

If choral speech is new to the school, start with a few children and work up to larger groups as experience and confidence increases. Less than ten children and more than twenty-five tends to be impractical, but the teacher's knowledge of the children concerned and their capabilities will obviously govern how many participants are used.

If care is taken to blend and harmonise voices this should give depth and colour to the performance. It should be ensured that no one child has a markedly stronger voice than the others. Clarity, diction and projection are important but so is harmony. Projection should not be confused with shouting. Children should be encouraged to speak normally but clearly, addressing their words to the back of the hall.

By learning the passage and concentrating on cue lines, phrasing and expression the children are encouraged to consider the meaning of the lines they speak. And they will not readily forget passages prepared in this way.

Choral speech can be further enhanced by the use of musical instruments. Use of drum beats, tambourines or short recorder melodies can be very effective. Silence is also very effective.

Children should be encouraged to keep relaxed but still during such a performance, so make sure they are given positions which are comfortable for them to hold for the length of the performance.

But I teach in a multi-faith school

Many of our large city schools these days have children from many different cultures, and therefore, potentially at least, from many different religions. Will these assembly outlines be relevant to children whose families are Muslims, Jews, Hindus, Buddhists and many others? Do we have the right to expect such children to take part in, and listen to these Bible-based assemblies?

I believe that there are several reasons why we not only have the right but also the duty to provide Bible teaching such as this in our Junior schools today. While children from Jewish and Muslim backgrounds will probably be familiar with much of the Old Testament material, albeit possibly in a different form, we should take care to respect the wishes of parents with regard to this matter.

For children from other cultures to understand and accept ours, they will need to have some understanding of the religious background of this culture. Much of our moral, literary and artistic heritage owes a lot to Christian ways of thinking. The Christian tradition has to a certain extent moulded the society we live in today. Children coming from other cultures with their own religious traditions, will be better able to understand life in this country if they understand something of the religion that has been part of life here for so long.

In any coming together of two different ways of life, there must be a mutual openness to the differences. Each side must try to see things from the viewpoint of the other. If we are to try to accept and share in the viewpoints and cultures of these children, cultures which offer a great deal to enrich our school life, we must be prepared to share ours too. Also, in trying to be fair to children from other races, we must not deprive our own of their heritage.

Many of the assemblies in this book, though using biblical material, make a point that is acceptable to all cultures; for example, that sharing, helping, giving, are all good things to be encouraged, while greed and selfishness should be avoided. These truths are ones which children from all over the world need to learn.

Finally, a Christian teacher, while respecting that her children have the right to disagree with her on matters of faith, will inevitably want to share with them some of the interesting, exciting, or touching things she has found in the Bible.

Using the outlines with small numbers and little space

On reading through these outlines you will find that they have been compiled with the idea of trying to include all the children in a class in the giving of an assembly. In many cases the staging diagram implies plenty of room for the children to move about. However, in some smaller schools there is just not enough space for this kind of action, and not enough children to fill all the parts needed and still leave some to watch.

These assemblies assume that you will want to involve a full class of about thirty children all of the same age, but of course in the small school there are just not this many children available. There are simple ways to adapt most of these assemblies for use with smaller numbers. In most cases where large numbers are needed, such as 'The Lame Man', 'Joshua', 'Noah', the majority of children will be 'crowd' or something similar, with no actual speaking parts as such. These parts can be taken by the children who are watching, given the odd word of guidance by the teacher. This will mean that they feel fully involved with what is going on, and the assembly will become more spontaneous and real to all concerned.

In many cases, too, the outlines assume that different children will be reading prayers, or showing pictures to those who are acting. This need not necessarily be the case. In 'The Blind Beggar' or 'Hands' for example, the same children could show their pictures and then go on to act the story.

Where choral speaking is suggested, there may not be enough children for the numbers stated. In a small room, where audibility is not a problem, and there are not so many people watching, children will not be so shy, and perhaps each group part could be taken by a single child.

In some cases you may prefer to involve the whole school in the assembly, and perhaps invite parents as audience. The Harvest outline is one such. In this and other cases involving large numbers of children you will find that the different ages fit very well, as there are small parts for the younger ones, and more demanding parts for the other children. See 'David – God's choice for King' where the brothers actually need to be different sizes!

Where music is suggested, you may want to record the children playing or singing beforehand and play back the recording during the assembly. In a small room this is quite feasible, whereas the sound will probably not carry sufficiently well in a large hall without amplification.

The other drawback to a small school is often lack of space. You may have looked at the staging diagrams and thought, 'I could never do that in our small room.' However there are ways of using a small room creatively. The advantage of a small area for assembly is of course that the whole thing immediately becomes more friendly and informal. If you have a small hall, let the action take place in the centre; this will involve the audience, and with few children there is not the same difficulty in seeing what is going on. It also takes less room than having a stage at the front.

If you have to have your assemblies in a classroom, the desks or tables pushed around the edge will provide seats for the watchers and can be used as staging to a certain extent. Most of the staging ideas have been kept quite simple, but all are no more than suggestions. Adapt what is given to fit in your rooms. You may find that rehearsals develop a suitable staging without much thinking about it.

To sum up, although you may have to adapt some of these outlines, it is hoped that you will find they fit into the small school situation very well. Consisting as many of them do, of several ideas put together into one integrated outline, you are free to include what fits your situation, and leave out anything else.

SECTION 1: OLD TESTAMENT

1 Obedience : Adam & Eve

AIM

To show that obeying God is the best way even though it is not always the easiest way.

BIBLE BASE Genesis 3:1–13

Adam and Eve were the first people in the wonderful new world that God had created. They had been provided with all that they needed physically, mentally and spiritually. Because they lived in perfect harmony with their Creator, they lived completely fulfilled lives, until the thought was planted in Eve that God had kept something back from them, and she allowed the thought to grow into a real temptation.

Not content with doing wrong herself, Eve had to involve Adam. The children will probably recognise themselves here; and every teacher knows that a gang of children will get up to far more mischief than one child alone; they 'egg each other on'.

Eve did not want to take the blame, and so disobedience was followed by dishonesty.

This story of the coming of evil into the world is also a picture of our situation today, and the children will be able to identify with it.

CLASS PREPARATION

Provide the children with mirrors and ask them to study their faces and then draw or write what they see. If not enough mirrors are available the children could draw each other. This will give you a 'rogues gallery' to display. A few days later ask if these pictures and writing give any idea what the children are really like. Help the children to see that it is what we are like 'inside', our thoughts and personality, that are the real 'us'. Let the children write about 'What I'm really like'.

Is what we let other people see, what we are really like? Often we can fool others about what we are like, and sometimes we can even fool ourselves, but God knows what we are really like. When we make excuses, and try to justify something that we know really was wrong, we are trying to hide even from ourselves what we are really like. There is a story in the Bible about people like that, too. Read or tell the story of Genesis 3:1–13.

Participants: *Acting* – A, B, C, D, Narrator, Woman, Man, God, Snake. The rest of the class will have their 'portraits' on display.

Props: Mirror for B, smaller mirror for C, Bible for D.

PRESENTATION

Hymn: 'God is love' (Sing to God 10)

A What are you doing?
B I'm looking at myself. I thought I had a spot on my chin. (*to C*) What are you doing?
C I'm looking at myself. I'm trying out a new hairstyle. (*to D*) What are you doing?
D (*Looking up from her reading*) I'm looking at myself, too.
A What do you mean? You're reading a book.
D In this book there are stories that make me see just what I'm like myself. This one at the beginning, for instance:–

(*Genesis 3 1–13. It is suggested that the story is read, not acted, but encourage the children to put lots of expression into what they are saying.*)

Narrator	Now the snake was the most cunning animal that the Lord God had made. The snake asked the woman:
Snake	Did God really tell you not to eat fruit from any tree in the garden?
Woman	We may eat the fruit of any tree in the garden, except the tree in the middle of it. God told us not to eat the fruit of that tree or even touch it; if we do, we will die.
Snake	That's not true: you will not die. God said that, because he knows that when you eat it you will be like God and know what is good and what is bad.
Narrator	The woman saw how beautiful the tree was, and how good its fruit would be to eat, and she thought how wonderful it would be to become wise. So she took some of the fruit and ate it. Then she gave some to her husband and he also ate it. As soon as they had eaten it they were given understanding, and realised that they were naked; so they sewed fig leaves together and covered themselves. That evening they heard the Lord God walking in the garden, and they hid from him among the trees. But the Lord God called out to the man:
God	Where are you?
Man	I heard you in the garden; I was afraid and hid from you because I was naked.
God	Who told you that you were naked? Did you eat the fruit that I told you not to eat?
Man	The woman you put here with me gave me the fruit, and I ate it.
God	Why did you do this?
Woman	The snake tricked me into eating it.

(A, B, C and D come forward)

D You see, that's just what I'm like sometimes. I don't do as I'm told, and then I blame it on somebody else.

A Well, Eve was tempted by the serpent. He was so nice to her.

D But she could have said: 'No, I trust God and will obey Him.'

B Adam only ate it when Eve gave it to him.

D But he knew he shouldn't. He could have said: 'No, I *will* do what I'm told.'

C It isn't always easy to obey. And sometimes it doesn't seem important.

D But it's the best thing to do in the end. Look at all the misery that's caused because people don't do what God says.

C Then I suppose we ought to try to obey, but how do we know what God says nowadays?

D He still speaks through this Bible. It tells us what God said we ought to do. Let's try and remember that every day. We can say a prayer now:

Prayer: Lord, teach us your way. Help us to obey you, for the sake of Jesus Christ our Lord. Amen.

Hymn: 'The Best Book to read is the Bible' (Sing to God 167)

FOLLOW-UP

1 Read the rest of the story in Genesis 3:14–24 to find out what happened to Adam and Eve.

2 Read other stories in the Bible of people behaving like we do. 1 Kings 19:1–10 – Elijah feels fed up. John 20:19 – Disciples are afraid.

3 Let the children make up playlets and act out situations where they are making excuses for something they have done wrong.

4 Let the children think about the Garden of Eden and what it was like. Can they draw or write about it? Look up Isaiah 65:17–25, Revelation 21: God promises that one day things will be like that again.

See also outline 2.

2 Obeying God:Noah

AIM

To show that it is important to obey God at all times even if others make fun of us.

BIBLE BASE Genesis 6:1 – 9:17

There is a great deal of material here so you will need to summarise much of it in your preparation.

The ark was huge (450 feet long), and to a people who had never seen the sea it must have looked grotesque.

The flood was a catastrophe unsurpassed either before or after. There are disagreements about how extensive it was, but the important thing for us is to tell the story as an incident of unquestioning obedience to God. (See 'The Genesis Flood' by Whitcomb and Morris for more detail.)

CLASS PREPARATION

Children are well aware of the bad things that happen in the world. Ask your class to tell you some of the bad things that have happened in the world in the past week. Violence, robbery and murder will probably be suggested. Ask the children why these are bad things. (Because they hurt people, make them unhappy.) Ask them to think about things they might have done which have hurt other people. Say that bad things like this hurt people but they also make God sad, because he wants to see people living good, loving and kind lives. Ask if it is always easy to be like this. Often it is easier to do things which we know are wrong, especially if other people make fun of us. The man in the story we are going to do for assembly must have faced a lot of ridicule. Tell the story of the building of the ark, and ask the children how they would have felt had they been asked to do such a thing.

Participants: *Acting* – Mrs Noah, Shem, Ham, Japheth, Noah, on-lookers, fighters, some children as animals. Choral speech: group of 4 upwards. The rest of the class will show paintings of the wrong things people were doing.

Props: Large painting of a rainbow, children's drawings of people fighting, arguing, stealing, a flower, large picture of an Ark, a few cut-outs of animals to be carried by children.

PRESENTATION

Hymn: 'And God said the sun should shine' (Come and Sing 3)

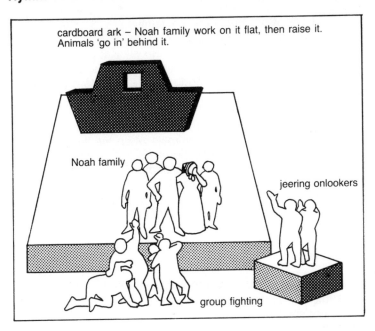

cardboard ark – Noah family work on it flat, then raise it. Animals 'go in' behind it.

Noah family

jeering onlookers

group fighting

Long ago God made a beautiful world. He made many lovely things, like this flower. But men spoilt God's lovely world by the bad things they did. They did all sorts of nasty things to hurt one another. (*Group mime fighting*). They told lies. They took things which did not belong to them. They lost their tempers. They hit each other and even killed one another. All this made God very, very sad. But there was one man, and his family, who *was* different. (*Show children's paintings as this is said.*)

Mrs Noah	I don't know what the world is coming to.
Shem	Everyone is fighting one another
Ham	Or telling lies
Japheth	Or stealing.
Mrs Noah	Where's father? We can't go on like this.
(enter Noah)	
Noah	Wonderful news! God has given me a special message today.
Mrs Noah	What did he say?
Noah	We are to build an ark – a great big boat.
Shem	Whatever for?
Noah	Because God is going to flood the whole world.
Ham	Who will go into the ark?
Noah	Just us – and lots and lots of animals.
Japheth	When shall we start?

| **Noah** | Right away – I'll get my tools. |

(*Noah and his family mime the building of the ark – cutting down trees, sawing, planing and hammering*)

Onlookers	
1	Look at old Noah and his family!
2	Whatever are they doing?
3	They say they are building an ark – a great big boat!
4	Whatever for? We are miles from the sea.
5	Because God is going to send a flood to drown us all – that's what Noah says – because we are so wicked.
6	I don't think God will, do you?
Noah	Well, at last we have finished. We have made a safe home for us and the animals when the flood comes.
Shem	Father! Look at those clouds!
Ham	The animals are coming, dad!
Japheth	We will have to sort them out.

(*Animal children go behind the ark, so only cut-outs are visible*)
And when they were all safe inside the ark; God closed the door.

Hymn: 'Noah was safe' (Come and Sing 51). The words could be mimed and/or sung.

When the flood was over, Noah, his family and all the animals came out of the ark. Noah thanked God for keeping them all safe. God made a very special promise:–

Choral speech:
'As long as the world exists, there will be a time for planting and a time for harvest. There will always be cold and heat, summer and winter, day and night.'

Prayer:
'Sorry' prayers for things we have done wrong.
'Praise' prayers for God's love and care.
God made another promise. He said he would never send such a flood again.
(*Show large 'rainbow'*)
When we see a rainbow in the sky it reminds us of God's promise.

Hymn: 'Who built the ark?' (Someone's Singing Lord 44)

FOLLOW-UP

1 There are all sorts of possibilities in art work: making models of the animals and the ark, painting, making a frieze of them all entering or leaving etc.
2 The ways these animals would have moved into the ark can be explored by pairs of children during movement lessons.
3 Imaginative writing could include children's ideas of what it would have been like in the ark, and the feelings the people must have

had when they were finally able to leave it. A 'diary' or 'log book' could be drawn up with all sorts of amusing incidents.

4 This particular story has been rewritten and put into pictures more perhaps than any other Bible story. There are several good picture books on the subject. Could the class read and compare some of these, with each other and with the original?

5 Science work on rainbows and the splitting of light.

6 Look up the stories of Daniel in the lions' den (Daniel 6:1–28), the fiery furnace (Daniel 3:1–30), Stephen's death (Acts 6:8 – 7:60) for other people who did what they knew to be right.

See also outline 1.

3 Moses : called by God

AIM

To show that we can do things which we think are impossible.

BIBLE BASE Exodus 3:1–4:17

As this is quite a long and complicated passage, much of it being in the form of a dialogue between Moses and God, it is suggested that you do not use all of it in your preparation with the class taking the assembly. However it could well be studied later, and the following guidelines may be of use.

Notice that Moses' interest was first aroused by the sight of this strange burning bush. He does not seem to have any inkling of what is to come.

The fact that Moses was told to take off his shoes, is related to the Israelites' view of God. They were very aware of the holiness of God, and their own sinfulness. This is something which modern society does not like to admit. Moses' taking off his shoes is a sign of submission and respect. Notice, too, that he is warned not to go too close, v. 5, as people thought that getting too close to God or his possessions would cause death. He also covers his face.

In verses 7–10 we are shown that God is involved in the life of his people.

The rest of the passage consists of a dialogue between Moses and God about whether or not Moses is 'the man for the job' – the 'job' in this case being to persuade Pharaoh to let the Israelites go and then to lead them out of Egypt and into the Promised Land. Moses is given plenty of proof that God really does know what he is doing. First the future is predicted for him, then he is given miraculous powers, and finally a helper.

CLASS PREPARATION

Ask the children if they have ever been asked to do something they thought was too difficult for them. How did they feel before and after doing it? Do they think adults ever have this problem? Can they think of things they might be expected to do as grown-ups that they would not want to do? The story for the assembly is about a man who did not really want to do a very important job.

Discuss the different kinds of jobs there are for grown-ups to do. If your class is suitable you may want to make a survey of fathers' jobs, and mothers' too. Be careful not to make those whose mothers do not go out to work feel strange; being a housewife is a full time job! Think about the different skills needed for the various jobs. Some people need to be able to drive, others need to be good at writing, or skilful with their hands. Some people do not meet many other people in their jobs, others are constantly meeting new faces. Discuss with the children the differing temperaments that make people suited for doing different things. They will be able to appreciate this in the classroom; there are some children who are good at sports, and others who enjoy singing. There are some who can be guaranteed to keep the class amused, while others are better at suggesting activities, or reading stories.

Point out that different jobs need different talents. Sometimes we do not know that we can do something, that we have the ability for it, until we are forced to do it, or try to do it. This is really what happened with Moses. He thought he could not do what God wanted; but God knew that he would be able to.

What sort of person do the children think would make a good shepherd? What about a diplomat? A prime minister? All these roles were fulfilled by one man – Moses.

Discuss with your class what jobs they might do when they grow up. Talk about the characteristics of doctors, nurses, policemen, and others which may be suggested. Select five children to mime their chosen occupations.

Participants: *Acting* – Moses, voice (concealed), sheep, several children to mime, children to read.

PRESENTATION

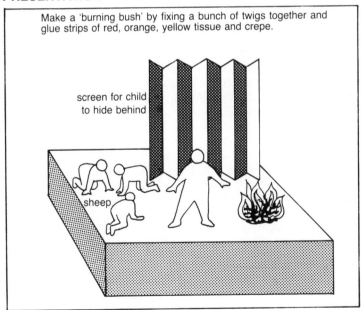

Make a 'burning bush' by fixing a bunch of twigs together and glue strips of red, orange, yellow tissue and crepe.

screen for child to hide behind

sheep

Hymn: 'When we walk with the Lord' (Hymns of Faith 414)

In our class we have been thinking about the different jobs people do.

These children are going to act, without using any words, what they think they might do when they have grown up.

(*As children do their miming let the children watching guess what jobs they are doing.*)

Different jobs need different skills. These children have thought about what they will need to know in order to do their chosen jobs. (*Four or five children read their thoughts on this subject.*)

The man in our story started as a shepherd, but God wanted him to do something quite different, something he thought he could not do. Watch!

(*One child to be Moses, others to be sheep and one, suitably concealed, to be the 'voice'.*)

Moses was in the desert, looking after his flock of sheep. Suddenly he noticed a burning bush. He expected the bush to burn up quickly. But instead it just went on and on burning. So he went to have a closer look.

When he got near the burning bush he heard a voice:

Voice   Moses, Moses!

Moses   Here I am.

Voice   Do not come near; put off your shoes from your feet, for the place on which you are standing is holy ground.

This was God speaking and Moses was afraid and hid his face.

God had a special job for Moses to do.

Voice   I want you to go to the King of the Egyptians and tell him to let my people, the Israelites, go. They have been slaves here long enough.

Moses   But I can't do that. I'm only a shepherd . . . the people wouldn't believe me. I'm no good at talking anyway, I'd get it all wrong. Please send someone else.

Voice   No, you are the one I want to do this job. But you can have your brother, Aaron, with you. He's good at talking; he'll help you.

            (*Moses turns away.*)

Voice   And, Moses, remember! I will always be with you too.

And Moses did go and tell Pharaoh to let the Israelites go, and the Israelites did listen to him and prepared for a journey. Moses didn't know he could do this very difficult job until he had tried it. It is just like that with us sometimes. When we are asked to do something new, we think we can't do it, that we'll do it all wrong, just like Moses did, but then if we take the plunge and have a go, we find it's not impossible after all. And God promised that he will be with us too, to help us if we ask him to.

Prayer:

Dear Lord Jesus,

Help us not to make excuses, like Moses, when we are asked to do something that seems difficult. Thank you that you will help us, when we ask you. Amen.

Hymn: 'Jesus' hands were kind hands' (Come and Sing 45)

FOLLOW-UP

1 Tell the story of Moses' birth and youth for those who do not know it (Exodus 2).
2 Make a frieze of pictures of the events in Exodus 3:1 – 4:17.
3 Make a tape-recorded paraphrase of the dialogue in Exodus.
4 Write poems about Moses' 'excuses' to God. What about times the children have tried to avoid doing something?
5 Read the account of the Exodus, i.e. the fulfilling of what God had said would happen. Let the children act it out, or do a frieze. Imaginative writing of all sorts could come out of this; poems about the events, 'diaries' of either an Egyptian or an Israelite, newspaper accounts for the 'Egypt Times'. (Exodus 7:14 – 13:22)
6 Using all this material make a book about Moses' life, or produce a 'This is your life'.
7 Read some of Moses' writing (he was a poet too), e.g. Deuteronomy 32:1–43.

See also the assembly outline on the giving of the Ten Commandments and the story of Moses' birth – outline 4, and also outline 36. Also outlines 6, 9 for other people God spoke to.

4 The Ten Commandments

AIM

To consider the guidelines God has given us so that we can lead the kind of life he created us to lead.

BIBLE BASE **Exodus 20:1–17.** The Ten Commandments
Mark 12:28–34. Jesus gives The Great Commandment
Deuteronomy 6:4–7; 30:11–15. The importance and relevance of the Law
Micah 6:6–8. True obedience

These passages are summaries of the way in which God wants his people to act. The two strands of love and worship towards God, and care and concern towards other people are closely interwoven, because in the Bible religion is seen as a part of daily life; the way we respond to God is reflected in the way we treat other people. To a certain extent this is always true; belief in a deity, or even in moral values will influence the way one sees other people. True worship, in the Bible, is always accompanied by love of one's fellow men.

CLASS PREPARATION

Ask the children if they have ever heard of the 'Ten Commandments'. What are they? Do the children know any of them? Where could they find them? You might want to explain them simply by saying that they are a set of rules for living that God gave the Israelites thousands of years ago, and which men today still hold to. Alternatively you could look them up in the Bible. Explain how they are divided into two sections: one showing a right attitude to God and the other a right attitude to other people. You may want to extend the material over two assemblies.

Go on to ask the children to think about what God wants people to do. How does he want us to behave today?

Tell the story in Mark 12:28–34, where Jesus summarises the law. Ask the children what they think it means to love God like that. Can they write poems about God and what he means to them? If they do not believe in God encourage them to write honestly about their thoughts on this subject.

Participants: *Acting* – Jesus, Teacher of the Law, Crowd, 10 readers. *Choral speaking* – 3 groups of 4 or more children, 1 solo. Other children will have written out the Ten Commandments for display during the assembly.

PRESENTATION

Hymn: 'Spirit of God' (Sing to God 102)

Prayer:
Lord God,
We know that you are a great God, but we also know that you care about each one of us. You want to be involved in our lives. You want us to be your friends and followers. Please show us how we can do what you want. In Jesus' Name. Amen.

We have been thinking about what God wants us to do. In school we have rules as guidelines to tell us how to behave. In the same way God gave his people, the Israelites, some rules or Commandments to tell them the best way to live.
Listen. (*Have the Ten Commandments written out in decorative writing on large sheets of paper and displayed at the front of the hall. Ten children could each read one, and point to it. Reference Exodus 20:1–17*).
These rules can be split into two halves; there are some which tell the people how to worship God (*the children could point to these*), and some which tell people how to behave towards each other. (*Point to the relevant ones again.*)

When Jesus was on earth, he was asked about these rules, or Commandments. Let's see what he thought about them.
Characters: Jesus, Teacher of the Law (*looking very proud and clever*), Crowd (*optional. You could use the readers from the previous part for*

this. Let the actors learn the words from Mark 12:28–34 and use only the dialogue in your playlet. Both Jesus and the teacher should turn towards the audience, as should the crowd when speaking, and should be chosen for their clarity of diction, as this is an important part of the assembly.)'

Jesus shortened the rules that we looked at earlier. He said we should love God and each other. (*You should ask the audience to supply the answers here.*) Think about this; when we really love God we are going to want to please him, and if we love other people too, as much as we love ourselves, we won't want to hurt them either. Let's sing a hymn about that.

Hymn: 'Lord of the Loving Heart' (Sing to God 122)

To finish our assembly we would like to read you some other parts of the Bible which tell us about what God wants us to do.

Choral speech: Three groups of not less than four children, solo

Group 1	The command that I am giving you today is not too difficult or beyond your reach. It is not up in the sky. (*Speakers all raise one arm as if pointing, and look upwards.*) You do not have to ask. . . .
Group 2	Who will go up and bring it down for us so that we can hear it and obey it?
Group 1	Nor is it on the other side of the ocean. (*Speakers point over the heads of the audience and shade their eyes as if looking into the distance.*) You do not have to ask. . . .
Group 3	Who will go across the ocean and bring it to us, so that we may hear it and obey it?
Group 1	No, it is here with you.
All	Remember this.
Group 1	The Lord, and the Lord alone is our God.
Group 2	Love the Lord your God with all your heart,
Group 1	with all your soul,
Group 3	and with all your strength.
Group 2	Never forget these commands that I am giving you today. (*Pause, while the speakers stand with heads bowed as if thinking about what has been said. Alternatively they could turn to look at the Ten Commandments as if reading them.*)
Solo	What shall I bring to the Lord, the God of heaven, when I come to worship him? Shall I bring the best calves to burn as offerings to him? Will the Lord be pleased if I bring him thousands of sheep or endless streams of olive-oil?
All	No (*Very loud*)
Group 1	The Lord has told us what is good. What he requires of us is this:

Group 2   To do what is just,
Group 3   to show constant love,
Group 1   and to walk in humble fellowship with our God.
(*Taken from Deuteronomy 29:29; 30:11–15; 6:4–5; Micah 5:6–9.*)
Now let us sing our final hymn.
Hymn: 'For your holy book we thank you' (Sing to God 165).

FOLLOW-UP

1 Let the children write our their own 'ten commandments'. What do they think is important for them? Compare these with the originals.
2 Read the story of the giving of the commandments. Exodus 19.
3 Read some of the parts of the Bible where the people of Israel admit to having failed to keep these laws. e.g., Isaiah 59.
4 If the children are able to cope with the idea, point out that since no one has ever managed to keep all of the laws all of the time, God made another way for us to get right with him. References to include are Isaiah 53, Romans 3:9–26.
5 Look up what Jesus said about the Old Testament law. Matthew 5:17–20.
6 Let the children choose one commandment to write out and illuminate.

Other outlines on Moses are 3 and 36. On 'What the Bible tells us to do', see outlines 1 and 21.

5 Joshua and the Battle of Jericho

AIM

To encourage children to think about the importance of working together as a team.

BIBLE BASE Joshua 5:13–6:22

This is the story of the capturing of the first city in the Promised Land. The land of Canaan had been promised by God to Abraham and his descendants over 700 years earlier. After the Israelites escaped from slavery in Egypt they wandered in the desert for forty years. Then they crossed the River Jordan, and set about defeating the inhabitants of the land that God had promised to give them. This battle is unusual because the city was taken without the usual siege and fighting. The success of the plan rested on all of the men obeying what might have seemed a ridiculous command, and working together.

CLASS PREPARATION

Take your class on to the playing field and get them to play a team game such as netball or football. After the game, discuss tactics and the need for teamwork. You may have examples of when they did not work together as a team and so the other side scored, or they may need to be congratulated on the way they worked together.

Ask them if they can think of other times when it is important for people to work together. An orchestra depends on all members following the conductor, an army depends on all soldiers obeying their commander. The children will probably be able to give you other suggestions. Ask them to imagine in each case what might happen if the team refused to obey and work together. Let the children write amusing stories about the disorganised army, the out-of-tune orchestra or the worst football team in the world.

Go on to say that each class in the school is a sort of team too. Think of times when you all need to work together and obey instructions without questioning them.

The story is about the unexpected results that happened when one particular army obeyed some very strange instructions.

Participants: *Acting* – 2 spies, Joshua, Angel, Narrator, Israelite army, priests, occupants of Jericho. Children to read prayers.

PRESENTATION

Hymn: 'In our work and in our play' (Sing to God 137)

Today we are going to think about working as a team and obeying instructions. Do you ever want to disobey the school rules? (*Give examples of your own rules here such as 'Do you think it would be more fun to run everywhere instead of being expected to walk?'*) But these rules are for a reason; to make school a safer, happier place and to allow all of us to work here together.

We have found a story in the Bible where it was very important that some soldiers obeyed what their commander told them to do, even though it probably seemed very silly to some of them. Watch while we act it for you.

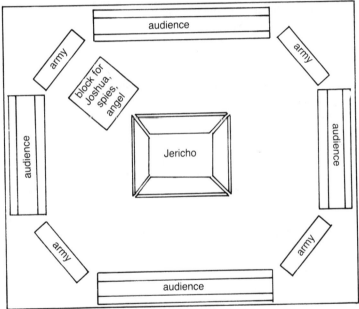

Use four sheets of card as walls – held up by the 'occupants' of Jericho and let go at the appropriate moment.

Spy 1	In Jericho's city over there, They're scared as mice, you've no idea.
Spy 2	They've shut their gate and locked their doors, They've got no heart to fight this war.
Joshua	I see and now I understand, It means that this is God's hand, The people are afraid of us in all this land. Well done, you two brave men Go back to your tents again. (*exit spies*)

	I must wait here and pray,
	For we must fight at break of day.
	(*Enter Angel with drawn sword*)
	Halt, who goes there? Are you friend or foe?
Angel	No, but I've come with this drawn sword,
	To be captain of the armies of the Lord.
Joshua	An angel of God! (*Falls flat on face*)
	What are your instructions?
Angel	First take off your shoes, for where you stand,
	Is not common ground, but holy land.
	Now listen while I give you your command.
	(*Joshua and Angel whisper together*)
Narrator	In the morning Joshua gave his plans for the battle to his men.
	(*Army assemble*)
Joshua	Men. Attention! (*Soldiers come to attention*)
	Now listen carefully to me.
	We've got to fight this enemy,
	No talking, let's get that straight,
	Whilst we are marching round this town
	You men are not to make a sound.
	The priests must blow their horns,
	Loud and clear!
	Now, quick march, you've nothing to fear!
Narrator	For six days they marched around the town, once each day.
	On the seventh day they went round Jericho seven times. All the time the priests were blowing their horns wildly. Then, at last. . . .
Joshua	Now is the time to capture this city,
	On everything living, take no pity,
	Except Rahab who helped the spies,
	Now let them hear your cries! Shout!
All	Hosannah!
Joshua	Shout!
All	Hosannah!
Joshua	Shout, shout, shout!
All	Hosannah! (*Walls fall down. Army goes in. Struggle*)
Narrator	With the shouting of the people the walls of Jericho fell down, and the city was swiftly captured. Joshua's army went on to conquer all the promised land in the days and years that followed the battle of Jericho.

You see, if the soldiers had not done exactly what Joshua said, they would not have been able to capture the city of Jericho. It was because Joshua could rely on his army to do what he said, and to work together as a team that the Israelites captured the city. We have been thinking about being reliable and have written some poems and prayers about teamwork. Listen to some of them now (*two or three children to read theirs*).

Hymn: 'Heavenly Father' (Sing to God 127)

FOLLOW-UP

1 Read in the next part of Joshua (ch. 7) what happened when the Israelites didn't obey what God had told them to do, and one man started disobeying the rules. You might like to work out a play for acting in another assembly about this.
2 Play all sorts of team games, not just sports ones, to encourage the children to think as a team, e.g. 1) finding small words in a big one. 2) working out a problem as a team. 3) quizzes. 4) how many different uses for a paper clip can you think of?
3 Could you get a soldier to come in and talk about the army to the children?
4 Form a class orchestra, and have various 'conductors'. Does it make a difference who is conducting?
5 Think about obeying your instructions and discuss class discipline.
6 Find out about warfare in Bible times. How would the people normally have gone about trying to capture a city?
7 Find out about the kind of city Jericho would have been. Talk about walled towns in general. Are there any remains near enough to go and visit? Why don't we build towns inside walls now? Make a model Jericho.

See outline 30 for the previous part of the story of the Israelites.

6 Samuel: the child who heard God's voice

AIM

To show that everyone, even young children, can love God and follow him.

BIBLE BASE 1 Samuel 3

Samuel grew up to be the last of the great judges in Israel. He anointed Saul to be the first king, and later David. The Jews had a special place where they worshipped God at Shiloh. Eli was the priest in charge of the Tabernacle and a Judge of Israel.

CLASS PREPARATION

Ask your children how they learn things. Some things, like words, they learn by seeing, or reading, other things they learn because someone tells them. Other things again, they learn by doing, such as PE skills. So there are many ways that information from outside gets into them. Ask them how they think God communicates with people. Use their suggestions in your assembly. He gives us beautiful things to look at, which tell us about his beauty and goodness. We learn about him by the things other people do; even a telling off can remind us that God has rules he wants us to keep. We often think about God when we hear a beautiful piece of music. But he has given us one very special thing that tells us about him. What is it? (the Bible). Once in a while though, God speaks to people so that they can actually hear him. He did this to a boy called Samuel. Read or tell the story.

Participants: *Acting* – Eli, Samuel, Narrator, Voice of God, children with pictures of beautiful things, children with objects, children to read prayers.

PRESENTATION

Today we are going to look at a story in the Bible about a little boy. Some people think the Bible is a book just for grown-ups and that children are too young to understand it. Some people think that God can be understood only by grown-ups and that children are too young to know him. And yet Jesus loved being with children and he always had time to talk to them. We're going to act a story about one young boy whom God spoke to. It's about a boy called Samuel. His mother had prayed for a son, and when Samuel was born, his parents promised that he would work for God as soon as he was old enough. So about the age you first started school, Samuel went to live in the Tabernacle with the priests and helped them.

Play:
Characters: *Eli, Samuel, Voice of God (off-stage), Narrator(s). Let the narrator read through 1 Samuel 3. Eli and Samuel should learn their parts by heart, and their cues, or let other children read these and let the actors mime.*

During the reading, Samuel and Eli are in their beds, which should be raised so that all the audience can see, as there is not much action. Samuel could sit up and rub his eyes each time he hears the voice, before getting up and running to Eli. Eli can make a big thing of settling down to sleep again each time, turning over and rearranging his covers.

Well, you may be thinking 'God never comes and talks to me like that.' Don't worry! You're not the only one, because God doesn't very often talk to people out loud so they can hear him with their ears. And yet God still speaks to people today – including children. So how does he do it? Well God knows that the best way he can get through to us is not by speaking in our ears but to our hearts.

When we say that God speaks to our hearts we do not mean the pumping machine inside us that sends blood round our bodies, but the real person inside, the real you who thinks and feels and decides. Sometimes he does it when we hear a beautiful piece of music or when we suddenly catch a glorious scent of roses. Or it might happen as we watch a fantastic sunset, or look up at the moon and stars on a clear night. God can also speak to us through other people when they take care of us and look after us and even when they have to tell us off. But the clearest way that God speaks to us is through the Bible, because when we read it he shows what he is like and what he has done for us in sending his son.

(As you mention the various ways God speaks to people, children could hold up pictures of the things mentioned or the object itself.)

In our class we have been thinking about things that we really enjoy seeing, the beautiful things that are there if we really look, and the things we really enjoy hearing and doing. All these things were given to us by God for us to enjoy. We have written prayers about them. Listen as we talk to God now.

Prayer: (Four or five children's prayers.)

Hymn: 'I'm very glad of God' (Someone's Singing Lord 22)

FOLLOW-UP

1 Play a majestic slow movement of classical music and ask the children to write down their thoughts as they listen. Suggestions: Bach's 'Air on a G string'. 'Adagio in G minor for strings and organ' by Albinoni.

2 Ask the children to write about any experiences which have made them think about God. These may be sad or happy or exciting.

3 Read in 1 Kings 19:9–13 how Elijah discovered what God's voice is really like. Elijah had to listen carefully to hear God's voice.

4 Talk about listening or refusing to listen to the voice of conscience within.

5 Read 'The Tanglewoods' Secret' by Patricia St John (Kingfisher Books) as a serial.

See outline 3 – where God speaks to Moses. Other 'child' assemblies are outlines 7, 15 and 36.

7 David: God's choice for king

AIM

God sees what we are really like and is always willing to forgive us.

BIBLE BASE 1 Samuel 16:1–13

In response to Israel's demand for a king, Samuel the prophet had anointed Saul to be their first king but Saul disobeyed God and was rejected by him. (See 1 Samuel 15.) Now Samuel is instructed to anoint someone else to be the future king.

CLASS PREPARATION

Ask the children to choose between two objects, one attractive outside but not so good inside, the other boring on the outside but with something exciting in it – for example, a brown paper parcel with a big toy in it, and a pretty parcel full of old newspaper. Ask them what they based their choice on. Was it the right thing? If not, why not? Explain that things are often not what they seem to be. There are several fairy stories which explore this theme, and the hero always chooses the right object, and gets the prize. You might like to search through a book of fairy stories and read some to your class.

Talk about the way people pretend to be what they are not. Some of these ways are quite harmless, like a woman who carefully puts her make-up on and curls her hair when she is going out to a party. And we all like putting on our best clothes sometimes. But we can pretend to be different from what we are like inside. Even if we do this, God knows what we are really like. Tell the story. Ask the children why they think God chose David rather than his brothers. Discuss their answers.

Participants: *Acting* – Samuel, Jesse, 7 sons, David, city leaders, messenger. Children for choral speaking – 2 groups.

Props: Small bottle for olive oil. Signpost for Bethlehem. Walking stick for Samuel, and large handkerchief. Crook and toy lamb for David.

PRESENTATION

Today's assembly is about choosing. I wonder how good you are at choosing. Suppose you had to choose who was to be the next king or queen of England. I wonder who you would choose and why. Would it be a good choice? Let's see how good you are at choosing things. (*Have concealed to show at this point two bowls; one must be shiny, decorative and beautiful on the outside, but inside it should contain an assortment of 'nasty' objects – e.g. plastic spiders, used tea-bags etc. The other must be old and dirty on the exterior (perhaps an old flower pot), but full of shiny necklaces and sparkling treasures.)*

Now, if I said you could have everything inside one of these bowls, which would you choose? Hands up who would choose this one? And this one?

(Reveal the contents of each bowl, lifting the items out one by one with tweezers.)

Perhaps it's just as well some of you are not choosing the next king!

Samuel, here, has to do just that, let's see if you can guess who will be chosen.

In this story God chooses the king and surprises Samuel by his choice.

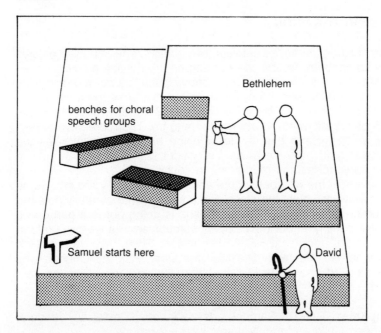

Play:
Characters: *Narrator (who reads the narrative and the voice of God), Samuel, Jesse, seven sons (going down in height), David (smaller than all the others), city leaders, messenger.*
Action. *The words can be learnt directly from the Bible passage, 1 Samuel 16:1–13, as can the narrative.*

Samuel is on stage with bottle of oil. He is joined by the leaders. When Jesse presents his sons they come forward one by one and in each case Samuel could raise the bottle of oil before lowering it slowly as if disappointed. After all seven, a messenger is sent for David.

Well, I wonder if you guessed right, or if you were surprised like

Samuel and Jesse. Samuel thought God would be sure to choose Eliab, Jesse's oldest son. Can you remember why? (Read v.6–7.) Samuel was looking at the outside of him, but God was seeing right into his thoughts. And he knew that Eliab would not make a good king. Instead he chose the youngest son of all, the one that Jesse had forgotten all about. And he didn't choose him for his looks or his nice eyes. He chose David because he knew that David looked good on the inside. David knew God and trusted him and obeyed him and that was why he would make a good king. It didn't matter to God whether he was as tall as his brothers; that was not important.

Sometimes we get a bit fed up with what we look like, don't we? Maybe you have said to youself, 'I wish I didn't have ears like this, or a nose like this'. Maybe you've looked at someone else and thought, 'If only I could look like that'. But when God looks at us it doesn't matter to him whether we have brown or red hair, whether it is curly or straight, whether our skin is black or white or whether we're tall or short, pretty or plain. He loves us just the way we are, because that's the way he made us. What he's really far more interested in is what we're like inside; whether we love him or not, whether we obey him by loving other people. God can see into the hearts of each one of us just as he could see into David's heart.

David knew that when he had done something that was 'nasty' inside he had to ask God to forgive him and make him all clean again. We are going to end now by using some of the words that David used when he was asking God to forgive him.

Choral reading:
(*Before this, tell the children that it is a prayer and so they can listen and if they agree inside with what the readers say, they can say 'Amen' at the end. Two groups of children.*)

Group 1   Be merciful to me O God,
               because of your constant love.
               Because of your great mercy, wipe away all my sin.

Group 2   Wash away all my evil and make me clean from my sin.
               Sincerity and truth are what you require; fill my mind with your wisdom.

Group 1   Remove my sin, and I will be clean,
               wash me and I will be whiter than snow.
               Create a pure heart in me O God, and put a new and loyal spirit in me.

All   Do not banish me from your presence.
               Do not take your Holy Spirit away from me.
               Make me willing to obey you.
               (*End like this:*)

Help us Lord today to have hearts that are clean and good, hearts that love you and obey you, so that we may please you as David did. Amen.

FOLLOW-UP

1 Write thank you prayers to God for making us special and different from anyone else.
2 Discuss the bowl illustrations and write down a list of things which spoil our lives. Turn the lists into 'sorry' prayers.
3 Read the parable of the Pharisee and the Tax-gatherer (Luke 18: 9–14). Get the children to write a modern version about two children going to church to pray. Which one was God pleased with?

Another 'choosing' assembly is outline 23.

8 Daniel

AIM

To encourage the children to stand up for what is right.

BIBLE BASE Daniel 6

Daniel was a Jew who had been taken into exile in Babylon. By his wisdom he had become an important man in the kingdom, so many of the native rulers were jealous of him. This story tells of their plot to get rid of him.

The plotters were unable to find anything that Daniel did wrong so they 'framed' him. Because he stood up for what he believed in, he got into trouble, but God was able to rescue him.

CLASS PREPARATION

Tell the children the story of a group of boys playing in the street one evening after school. They decided to have fun ringing doorbells and then hiding before the door was opened. It's a game that lots of children play, which seems to be fun, but can be very upsetting to the people inside the houses. One of the boys, Simon, said he thought it was a silly game. It had been done to his Granny a few weeks ago, and she had been very cross. He said he was not going to play and he didn't think the others should either. The other children just laughed at him. 'It's all right' they said, 'it doesn't hurt anyone. It's only a game.' When he still wouldn't join in they started to call him names saying he was 'chicken' and scared of being caught. Then they said he couldn't be in the gang any more if he didn't join in. This made him really sad. It would mean he'd be alone at playtimes, no more football in the park on the way home, no one to go swimming with on Saturdays. He hesitated. Then he made up his mind. 'It's still wrong,' he said. 'I'm going home.' And he walked off.

Ask the children if they have ever been told to stand up for what they believe is right. This is what Simon did. Explain that it is quite easy to say what you think when you know other people agree and will approve, but sometimes we find ourselves disagreeing with other people. The test of how brave we are, inside, is whether or not we change our minds to 'go along with the crowd'. In some places in the world people are in prison for thinking the 'wrong' thing. A similar thing happened to Daniel. Read or tell the story. Make sure the children realise that Daniel did not know that God would rescue him; what he did know was that God was able to if he wanted to.

Participants: *Acting* 3 princes, Narrator, Darius, Daniel, Guards, Lions (children could have cardboard masks). Children to read prayers.

PRESENTATION

Hymn: 'He who would valiant be' (Sing to God 155)

Have you ever heard someone say, 'Don't be afraid to stand up for what you believe is right'? What this means is that you really ought to be brave enough to say and do what you believe in, even if other people don't agree with you.

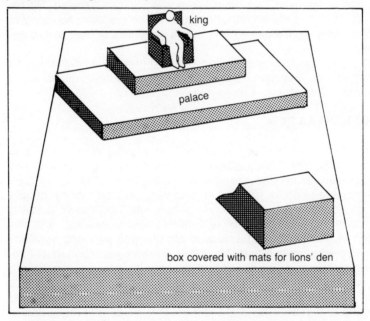

king

palace

box covered with mats for lions' den

Watch and see what happened to one man who stood up for what he knew was right, even though it would get him into trouble. He was a man called Daniel, and he lived in a city called Babylon. He hadn't been born there; he came from Israel, but the king of Babylon had captured Israel and taken many of the people who lived there back to his city. Daniel was a clever man who had helped the king, so he had been given a very important job to do, helping to rule the city. The princes of Babylon were jealous; they thought they should be the ones in charge. . . .

Prince 1   There he is. Just look at him. Daniel the Jew, ruler of Babylon.

Prince 2   I think this Daniel should be taught a lesson.

Prince 3   The harder the lesson the better. How can we have him punished?

Prince 1   I have watched him carefully. There is no law that he breaks. But what if we could trap him?

Prince 2	How?
Prince 1	He prays!
Princes 2 & 3	NO!
Prince 1	Yes! three times a day and out loud. (*Aside*) Work hard, Daniel. You will soon be going on a nice holiday to prison! Here is my plan. (*Whisper together. Exit all, Daniel last holding papers.*)
Narrator	The princes plotted to trick the King into making a new law. It was soon written and the King, knowing nothing of the plot, signed it. The law said: ANY MAN WHO PRAYS TO ANY GOD DURING THE NEXT THIRTY DAYS EXCEPT TO DARIUS THE KING SHALL BE THROWN INTO A DEN OF LIONS. When Daniel heard of the new law he did not stop praying to his God and it was not long before the Princes had ordered the Palace Guard to arrest him. (*Enter Darius who sits on throne*) So it was that one day, as Darius was on his throne, Daniel came in, a prisoner. (*Enter Daniel bound with 2 guards and princes*)
Darius	Daniel!
Prince 1	We have a law-breaker here, O King. He prays to his God and not to you and must be thrown to the lions.
Darius	Is it true, Daniel?
Daniel	It is true, O King.
Darius	My heart breaks for you. But I cannot save you from the lions. Our laws cannot be changed.
Prince 1	Guards! Throw Daniel into the den of lions!
Darius	Daniel, Daniel! May the God whom you serve, save you from the lions. (*Daniel thrown by guards into the lions' den. Exit princes*).
Narrator	That night the King was very sad. He would not eat. He would not drink. When they came to play music for him, he sent them away. There was no sleep for him that night. When morning came, Darius was up early and went quickly to the lions' den.
Darius	Daniel! Daniel! Has your God saved you from the lions?
Daniel	Do not be afraid, O King, the God that I serve has sent his angel to shut the mouths of the lions. They have not hurt me.
Darius	It's a miracle! (*Dances happily*) Quickly guards, let him out. (*Guards release him*)
Narrator	Then the king made a great announcement.
Darius	I, Darius, make an order that in every part of my kingdom men must tremble and fear the Living God who saved Daniel from the power of the lions.

So, there you are. Everyone thought Daniel would die but God looked after him.

Let us pray.

(*Children's prayers for people who are in prison because of what they believe, and for courage to be true to what we believe.*)

Hymn: 'Stand up, stand up for Jesus' (Sing to God 152)

FOLLOW-UP

1 Look up the other exciting story in the book of Daniel: the Fiery Furnace.
2 Talk about times when the children need to be brave; what things are they particularly scared of?
3 Find out about some of the dissidents and political prisoners in various parts of the world. Have a debate about whether people should be put in prison because of what they think. Include an example where they should.
4 Look up some of the people in the New Testament who suffered because of their faith in Jesus. Acts 7 – Stephen, Acts 12 – Peter, Acts 16:16–40 – Paul.
5 Talk about persecution of the early church by the Romans.
6 Let the children imagine themselves into the role of either the king or Daniel. What would their thoughts have been during the night when he was in the lions' den?

Another assembly about the 'impossible' is given in outline 9.

9 Never give up hope: Ezekiel

AIM
To show that with God we need never feel hopeless.

BIBLE BASE Ezekiel 37:1–10

In 597 BC the Babylonian army invaded Jerusalem and deported the king and thousands of leading men to Babylon. Ezekiel was a Hebrew prophet who was among those exiled in Babylon. He was used to God speaking direct to him, so he was very surprised when he felt God lead him to a valley where the ground was covered with human bones. Probably it was a battlefield where the bodies had been left and now after years of sun, storm, vultures and hyenas all that remained were dry bleached bones.

Ezekiel obeys God's commands and sees the bones come to life. So he is given a vivid promise for the renewing of the nation of Israel.

CLASS PREPARATION

Explain the historical background to the exile in Babylon. Discuss how the people felt as refugees – strange country and language. Link with the situation of refugees from Vietnam, Afghanistan etc. today. Talk about feelings of hopelessness. When do we feel hopeless? What do we hope for? The idea of hope should be within the children's own experience and not something abstract. What do they hope for tomorrow, at Christmas, next birthday, when they grow up? They can discuss a specific hope in small groups, and write about 'Next week' 'When I am 13' 'Tomorrow'.

If the children belong to an organisation, what plans are there for the future? Do they hope to go on a day outing, a camp, to a play or to the cinema? What preparation is needed? Who organises everything? This can be shown on a flow diagram with the object of emphasising that work is important to bring about the fulfilment of a hope.

our trip to the seaside

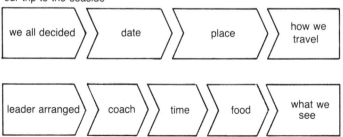

Participants: *Acting* – 7 narrators, Jews, Ezekiel, Dancers

PRESENTATION

A dance/drama

Narrator 1   The date is 590 BC. The place is Babylon – a land of canals, gardens and huge statues of gods and goddesses. The Babylonians are proud of their history, their land and their religion.

Narrator 2   The Jews who live in Babylon want to go back to their own country. (*Jews working on stage.*) The Babylonians had invaded their land and had taken them away as prisoners. They sit by the canals in the evening when they have finished their work and they sing. (Psalm 137). (*Jews sit down by river for chorus.*)

Chorus 1   'By the rivers of Babylon,
We sat down.

Chorus 2   There we wept,
When we remembered Zion.'

Narrator 3   They had no hope of ever going back home.

Narrator 4   One of the exiles was a man called Ezekiel. God often spoke to him. Sometimes God spoke to him in a vision. One day God told him he would give the exiles a new life. He would breathe new spirit into them and they would be new people.

Narrator 5   To show what he meant God took Ezekiel to a valley. (*Ezekiel crosses river to valley.*) This valley had once been a battlefield. Thousands of men had been killed there. Only their bones were left.

Narrator 6   God said, 'I will bring these bones back to life. Tell them what I said.'

Narrator 7   So Ezekiel told the bones to listen and obey.

The dancers have been lying scattered on the floor while the narrators have been speaking. As Narrator 7 speaks Ezekiel steps among the 'skeletons'. A tape of 'Dem bones, dem bones,' should be played, or a group of children could sing it. On the words, 'Now hear de word of de Lord', Ezekiel throws his arm wide and then retires into the background.

As the song goes through the different bones, the children move these parts. The whole dance should be jerky and spikey. Up to the hip bone the dancers may prefer to sit or lie but it is best to allow the children to use their discretion about when to get to their feet. The dance should be free and spontaneous. The song should only continue until all 'bones' are connected and then finish with the chorus.

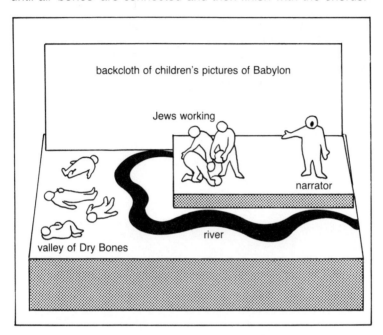

Ezekiel was given a vision by God to give him a hope to work for; something that had seemed impossible. He now knew that the exiles would be able to go back to their own land one day and so he began to do all he could to make that day come. Sometimes things seem impossible to us too, but we must try never to give up hope, and to work for what we hope for.

Prayer: Give us eyes to see,
                   And ears to hear,
                   And hands to do,
                   So that what we hope for may happen.

Hymn: 'I listen and I listen' (BBC Hymnbook for Junior schools)

FOLLOW-UP

1 Find out more about Babylon. Make a frieze about life in Babylon including the capture and deportation of the Hebrews.
2 Look up Ezekiel's other visions.
3 Look at pictures of skeletons of all sorts: animal, fish, bird, human. Collect bones: joints from chickens, knuckles and marrow bones

45

from the local butcher, fishbones. Clean, examine and draw them.

4 Perhaps a doctor, nurse or PE specialist could talk about the human skeleton, using children, slides and films.

5 Find out about 'skeletons' of non-living things. Make drawings and models (e.g. houses, ships, trees).

6 Talk about archaeology. Bones are very useful as archaeological evidence. Can the children find out why? It is also important to realise that bones are only part of the evidence for an archaeologist. Discuss what else he will use to help find him out about things.

7 The idea of hope can be introduced on a community level by the children making a list of things they would like to see changed in contemporary life, and then thinking what they can do about them.

10 Fair shares for all

AIM

To make the children aware of hunger and need in the world, and to stimulate them to think sympathetically and do something practical about the situation.

BIBLE BASE

While there is no Bible material actually included in the assembly outline, the theme is one which is found time and time again in the Bible. Such passages are given here for use either before or after the assembly with the children.

Amos 8:1–6 – Israel's cheating
Isaiah 10:1–2 – Injustice
James 2:1–9; 5:1–6 – Inequality of rich and poor

In each of these passages, notice that it is not merely that God does not want poverty, though this of course is true, but more importantly, that he does not want an unfair division of resources and possessions. And this of course is exactly the state of affairs in the world today.

You will need to be sensitive in using this outline with younger children.

CLASS PREPARATION

This assembly may well follow on quite naturally from a news broadcast or a newspaper report of some famine or disaster. The children could collect newspaper cuttings on the subject and add their own news articles and comments. Try to go into the causes of what has happened – natural disaster, earthquake, climatic conditions, fighting and so on. With older children look up the Bible references given.

A great deal of imaginative work can be done here. Let the children write and draw, especially trying to put themselves into the position of those affected.

Encourage the children to think about all the good things which they need and which they take for granted, things like enough water to drink and wash in, good wholesome food, grown-ups with time and energy to care for them in all sorts of ways. Poems and prayers on this subject could be written for inclusion in the assembly.

Participants: 7 rainbow children, 7 children of famine, children with prayers, optional group to sing (and play) 'I can sing a rainbow'. Cast: Seven rainbow children: red, orange, yellow, green, blue, indigo and violet, each dressed entirely in the appropriate colour, using ordinary clothes. Seven 'children of famine'; dressed in ragged tunics with bare arms and legs.

Record or song. 'I can sing a rainbow'.
(*Rainbow children step forward to say their lines, then stand back.*)

Red
Red is the colour of the sun, roses, poppies, ripe fruits, berries and the robin's breast.

Orange
Orange is the colour of marigolds and fire, carrots, goldfish and jaffa oranges.

Yellow
Yellow is the colour of ripe corn and autumn leaves, bananas and canaries.

Green
Green is the colour of leaves and grass, cabbages, moss and emeralds.

Blue
Blue is the colour of sea and sky, cornflowers, forget-me-nots and the blackbird's egg.

Indigo
Indigo is the colour of the raven's wing and the midnight sky.

Violet
Violet is the colour of grapes, amethysts, the tiny violet and the stately iris.

All
All the colours of the rainbow remind us of the richness of the earth.
(*Each child says his lines then comes and kneels in front of the rainbow child addressed.*)

1st child
For you, red means flowers and juicy fruit, but for me red means a scorching sun that bakes the earth hard and dry and shrivels the crops.

2nd child
For you, orange is a pretty colour reminding you of pleasant things, but for me orange means the colour of my little brother's hair. It was black, but now it has changed its colour because of disease, and his stomach is swollen with hunger. My little brother is dying.

3rd child
For you, yellow is the colour of corn waiting to be harvested. For me, yellow is the colour of the parched grass which will not nourish my cattle, and the seedlings that will only wither and die.

4th child
For you, green symbolises growing plants. It does also for me. But you see fertile fields and I see only barren wastes.

5th child
Blue is the sky above us both, but the sky over you drops rain. Above me there are no clouds of life-giving water.

6th child
Indigo shows for you the majesty of midnight but I feel only the blackness of despair in my heart.

7th child
For you, violet is a rich colour glittering in precious stones. But violet is also the colour of mourning and death and it is I that mourn and I that die.

Reader
'God said "I am putting my bow in the clouds. It will be the sign of my covenant with the world. . . . As long as

	the world exists, there will be a time for planting and a time for harvest. There will always be cold and heat, summer and winter, day and night.' Genesis 9:13; 8:22.
Children of famine	But, Lord, we die of hunger, and famine brings diseases and deformity.
1st child	Our wells run dry.
2nd child	Our cattle die.
3rd child	Our bones grow soft, and bend.
4th child	Our sight dims.
5th child	Our babies die first.
6th child	Our old people die next.
7th child	Our mothers weep.
Children of famine	The vultures come and feed on the bodies of our cattle, and only they grow fat.
Rainbow children	We are well fed and healthy, but often we are wasteful. God did not mean that any of his children should die in want, while a few live in luxury. But what can we do?
Red	We can give up our pocket money to help these people.
Orange	We can learn not to be greedy or wasteful.
Yellow	We can learn all we can, so that when we are grown up our knowledge can help others in need.
Green	We can pray for the people of other lands.
Blue	We can support missionaries and people who go to help them.
Indigo	When we are older, we can go ourselves to help.
Violet	We can learn to share what we have now.

Prayer: Forgive us, Lord, for accepting all your gifts without thinking. Help us to show our thanks by sharing what you have given us. Amen. (*Or use children's own prayers and thoughts here.*)
Hymn: 'Kum ba yah' (Sing to God 147).

FOLLOW-UP

1 Read the story of the giving of the rainbows in Genesis 8, 9.
2 Using the Bible passages given, let the children think about our own society. Are we guilty of the same faults? Let them be 'present day prophets' and write about it. Discuss waste and the consumer society. Encourage them to be more responsible with regard to the vanishing resources of the world. Think up alternatives for such things as the motor car, electricity, etc.
3 Make posters for display in school or elsewhere, to make people think about giving.
4 Sponsor a child in a developing country, through Tear Fund, 11, Station Road, Teddington, Middlesex, TW11 9AR. N.B.This is a

long-term project. This will provide on-going geography, letter writing, money-making, etc. It will also teach your children a lot about other people and the way they live.

5 Short term projects could include collecting money for one item of equipment needed in a developing country. Missionary societies will be able to give suggestions. The children could collect for a tractor for example, colouring in parts of a picture as they collect the needed money. Alternatively collecting foil for a guide dog for the blind or knitting squares for a blanket might be possibilities.

Other outlines along these lines are numbers 15 and 31.

11 Pattern

AIM

To encourage children to see, appreciate and care for design and order in God's creation.

BIBLE BASE Psalm 95:1–7

This passage has been selected to reflect the ideas in the assembly, showing pattern in words, and also appreciation of the order and consistency of nature.

CLASS PREPARATION

Discuss design in animal markings; this could follow from a visit to a zoo or farm, or from a programme on television. Get the children to collect pictures of patterned animals. Make large models for display during the assembly, either 3D, or card so that they will stand up, and use collage or painting techniques, e.g. sponge printing for spots, strips of paper stuck on for stripes.

Encourage the children to look closely at the pictures of animals they have collected, and to try to describe them in prose or poetry.

Look for other patterns in nature: pretty flowers, leaf clusters, snowflakes, etc., depending on the time of year.

Talk about the reasons for patterns in nature: camouflage, to attract a mate, to attract insects, and also because God created the world to be a beautiful place, reflecting the variety of his character.

Let the children experiment in making patterns. Some suggestions for use in the assembly have been given and you may want to include these or your class may come up with better ideas to use in the presentation.

Words can also form patterns. Read some poetry to the children to help them appreciate the beauty of words. Some of the most beautiful poetry is in the Bible. Prepare the passage for group speaking.

Participants: Children with animal models, children dancing – making 'body patterns', children to demonstrate art work patterns. Choral speakers: 12 children and musicians, children with prayers, musicians for closing music.

PRESENTATION

Hymn: 'If I were a butterfly' (Sound of Living Waters 106).

We have been singing about different animals. Our class has been thinking about patterns and we have made some large animals: stripy zebra, symmetrical butterfly, tiger (*add as many as you have, or have time for*).

Animals are often patterned for a special reason – protection and camouflage for example.

We have tried making patterns with our bodies. (*Children demonstrate, standing alternatively stretched and stooped, arms and legs wide etc.*)

We have also made patterns in our art lessons. We made potato prints, and patterns using doilies. (*Again demonstrate and add as many as you have time for. Remember to make them big. Additional material may be displayed on screens or walls throughout the assembly.*)

Everything you look at has patterns. Look closely at things in the classroom and in the playground to see: our eyes, fingerprint patterns, flower petals, rain in puddles.

God has made everything in so much detail. He made it for us to enjoy and to make us happy. These children are going to read a poem from the Bible about God, and the way he made everything. A poem is a word pattern. This one is also a prayer, because it is talking to God. Listen carefully.

Choral speaking: Psalm 95:1–7
(*Arrange the children who are doing the choral speaking in an attractive way, using forms or blocks to vary height, and have some standing, others sitting or kneeling.*

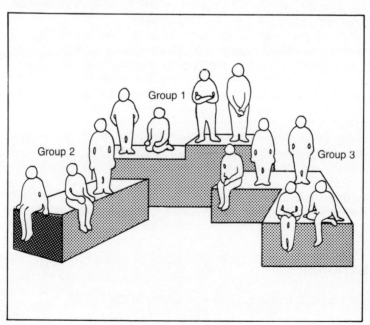

Musical instruments can be used to add liveliness to the psalm.
Group 1: four children.
Group 2: three children.
Group 3: five children.
Have a short recorder melody played as introduction, ending with a tambourine clash.)

Group 1   Come let us praise the Lord!
            Let us sing for joy to God, who protects us!
            (*Repeat introductory tune*)

Group 2   Let us come before him with thanksgiving, and sing joyful songs of praise.
            For the Lord is a mighty God, a mighty king over all the gods.

Group 3   He rules over the whole earth, from the deepest caves to the highest hills.
            He rules over the sea, which he made; the land also, which he himself formed.
            (*While group 3 are speaking these lines, appropriate quiet music could be played, deep drum beat for 'the deepest caves', glockenspiel notes for 'highest hills', rippling sounds for 'the sea', and perhaps bird sound for 'the land'.)*

Group 1   (*Suiting actions to words.*)
            Come, let us bow down and worship him.

Group 3   (*Suiting actions to words.*)
            Let us kneel before the Lord, our maker.

All   He is our God; we are the people he cares for, the flock for which he provides.

Prayer: We have written some thank you prayers for patterns.
    We must show God how grateful we are by really looking after this world he has given us and keeping it as he made it. So don't drop litter, don't pick flowers and spoil plants.

Hymn: 'Morning has broken' (Someone's Singing Lord 3)
    (*Children play rhythmic tune on recorders and percussion to make sound patterns as children go back to their classes.*)

FOLLOW-UP

1 More work on patterns of all kinds: tesselations and symmetry, number patterns in maths; collecting poems and tongue twisters; lots of art work; patterns using individual bodies, groups of children, and dance patterns in movement lessons.
2 Make posters about conservation, pollution, etc.
3 Look up other poetic portions of the Bible. You may want to introduce the Authorised Version here for the sound of the words, e.g. Psalms, Genesis 1, Isaiah 40; 43:1–7, Job 39–41.
Other assemblies about God's world are outlines 10 and 31.

SECTION 2: LIFE OF JESUS AND EARLY CHURCH
12 Lord of the dance

AIM

To give a general summary of the life of Jesus.

BIBLE BASE

The song 'Lord of the Dance' is a very popular one with children and it forms a useful introduction to the life and work of Jesus. Although there are no Bible passages as such used in the assembly itself, you will probably want to refer to some of the events in Jesus' life with the children either as part of preparation or as follow-up work. A list of references, which tally with the events in the song, is given here. It should be noted that these are not the only possible passages, and the song in fact would serve as the basis for a whole term's RE work on the life of Jesus if you wanted to use it in this way.

Verse 1 lines 1,2: Genesis 1:1–19, John 1:1–5.
        lines 3,4: Matthew 1:18–2:12, Luke 2:1–21.
Verse 2 lines 1,2: Matthew 15:1–9, Mark 2:1–12; 12:13–17.
        lines 3,4: Mark 1:14–19.
Verse 3 to 'Sabbath' Mark 3:1–6.
        to 'lame' Luke 13:10–17, John 5:1–18.
        line 3: Luke 6:6–11.
        to 'stripped' Mark 15:15–20.
        to end Matthew 27:32–56.
Verse 4 to 'down' Matthew 27:57–61, Mark 15:42–47.
        to 'high' Mark 16:1–7, John 20:1–29, Acts 1:6–10.
        lines 2,3,4: John 11:20–27; 15:1–10.
The song will be found in 'Faith, Folk and Nativity', Galliard.

CLASS PREPARATION

If the children do not already know the song, teach it to them and add any accompaniments that you want to include for the assembly. You will need to sing it quite slowly to allow all the action to take place.

Ask the children what they think the song is about or, if they find this difficult, ask why some people have thought it is about Jesus. They could make lists of the events mentioned in the song. Can they list the important events in their own lives in the same way, and perhaps turn them into a song or poem?

Discuss with the children the reason for putting such events in a song. Originally folk songs, of which this is a modern example, were a king of 'audio-aid' for a population who on the whole could not read and where, in any case, there were very few books. Adding a dance to the song, as you are going to do, is in the same tradition. It is a sort of 'learning made easy'. The children may be able to think of other ways of getting a message across without using the written word.

You may want to look up, or to tell as a series of 'story times', the main events referred to. (see Bible Base)

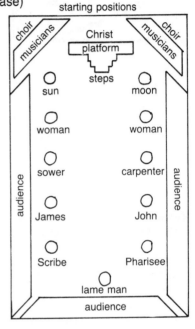

starting positions

PRESENTATION

Participants: *Dancers* – Jesus, sun, moon, carpenter, sower, James, John, Scribe, Pharisee, two women, lame man.

choir
musicians
rest of class

other movements – followers – – →

Christ figure's movements ➤ ➤ ➤

Scribe and Pharisee > > > >

(*Setting: Christ figure stands on platform with back to the audience. The other dancers kneel opposite each other with heads touching the ground and arms curved over heads, not moving.*)

Musical Introduction

Verse 1
I danced in the morning when the world was begun,
(*Christ figure turns to face audience and moves to the dancers.*)
And I danced in the moon and the stars and the sun.
(*He gently touches first the moon, then the sun, who uncurl and rise. The sun spreads out arms and the moon raises one arm in a curve over the head holding the other in a downward curve to the side. They turn slowly from the waist from side to side.*)
And I came down from heaven and I danced on the earth
At Bethlehem I had my birth.
Chorus
(*Christ moves along the line of dancers touching each in turn. The women kneel up; one mimes sewing, the other grinding corn. The sower mimes sowing seed. The carpenter stands and imitates sawing wood. The fishermen stand and mime casting nets. The Scribe and the Pharisee stand with arms folded and regard the others with a superior air. The lame man rises and sits with one leg folded under him, holding out one hand as if begging.*)

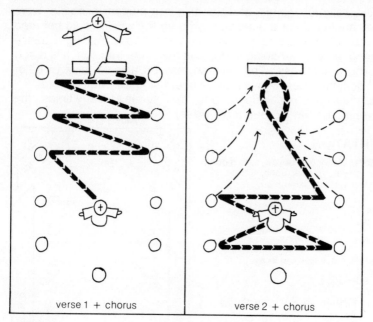

verse 1 + chorus   verse 2 + chorus

Verse 2
I danced for the Scribe and the Pharisee,
(Christ approaches first the Scribe, then the Pharisee, holding out hands in an appealing gesture, and beckons them to come.)
But they would not dance and they wouldn't follow me,
(Scribe and Pharisee turn away from Christ with angry gestures of rejection and angry looks.)
I danced for the fishermen, for James and John,
They came with me and the dance went on.
(Christ figure moves sadly away from the Pharisee and on to James and John. He beckons to them and they drop their nets and follow Christ, who moves back up towards the platform.
Chorus.
(At 'I'll lead you all', Christ figure turns and comes towards audience again. As he passes them the women, carpenter and sower all stop their work and follow.)

Verse 3
I danced on the Sabbath and I cured the lame,
(Christ figure approaches the lame man who leans towards him holding out his arms. Christ grasps his arms and pulls him to his feet. The lame man leaps upwards.)
The holy people said it was a shame.
(Scribe and Pharisee move swiftly forwards and grasp the Christ figure. They swing him round angrily to face the platform.)
They whipped and they stripped,
(Christ figure takes long staggering steps to the platform followed by

*the others who take long stamping steps and mime whipping. The
fishermen, and lame and blind men follow sadly.)*

And they hung me high
And left me there on a cross to die.
*Christ figure turns, mounts steps to platform, turns and holds out his
arms, sagging forwards from the waist as if hanging on a cross.)*
Chorus. *(sung softly)*
*(Dancers turn and move slowly back to starting positions with heads
bowed, all except James and John who go forward and kneel on one
knee with heads bowed facing Christ. Sun and moon stand with heads
bowed and arms folded across chest.)*

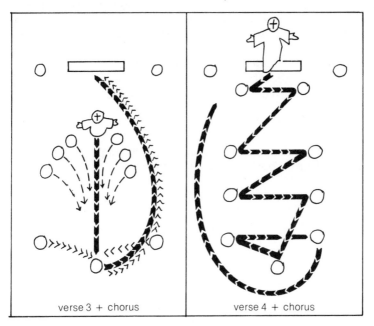

| verse 3 + chorus | verse 4 + chorus |

Verse 4
They cut me down,
(Christ figure bows down from the waist.)
and I leapt up high,
(He straightens up and lifts arms high above his head.)
I am the life that'll never never die,
*(He moves down and takes James by the hand, raising him up. James
rouses John and with Christ leading they dance down between the
rows of dancers who join on to make a chain of dancers. As the chain
passes by the Scribe and Pharisee they turn and look longingly after
the happy people passing by.)*
I'll live in you if you'll live in me
*(Christ leaves the rest and goes back to the Scribe and Pharisee. He
holds out his hands as if to welcome them. They look at him, then at
each other, then back at him, and run to him.)*

I am the Lord of the dance said he.
(All re-form chain, and dance around and off during singing of final chorus. At this point you may want to have a teacher explaining that the song and dance the audience have just watched is a picture of Christ's life. It would be more effective, however, if the assembly ended at this point and the children were sent back to their own classes to discuss with their own teachers what the actions were all about.)

FOLLOW UP

The children should be encouraged to tell you what they thought of the assembly, especially if they are not used to this sort of presentation.

Look up the stories suggested in Bible Base which give some of the incidents on which the song is based. Make a frieze of the events given.

Discuss with the children why Jesus is called the 'Lord of the Dance' (this is not a biblical title). What other names is he given in the Bible and elsewhere? (e.g. Son of Man, Messiah, Holy One of Israel, Christ, Son of David)

Do you or the children know other folk songs like this one? Could you start a collection, perhaps copied out and illustrated, and with percussion parts written for them. A book which might help here is 'Faith, Folk and Clarity' published by Galliard.

See the other outlines in this section (except 20, 21) for more detail on the life of Jesus – also 32, 33, 34, 35.

Other musical outlines are numbers 30, 31, 32, 37.

13 Friends

AIM

To stimulate children to think about friendship.

BIBLE BASE

Matthew 4:18–22. Jesus calls four fishermen.
Luke 5:27–32. Jesus calls Levi, the tax-collector.
John 1:40–42. The first disciples of Jesus.

When Jesus' 'inner band' of friends was complete, it consisted of twelve men, see Matthew 10:1–4. These were his close friends – though of course there were many others who followed him, as stories such as the sending out of the seventy-two (Luke 10:1–20) show.

In our passages here it seems very unlikely that Jesus called any of these people to follow him without any preparation. Indeed the passage from John's Gospel shows that some of them at least had been disciples of John the Baptist first, and so they would have heard about Jesus from him. Jesus had been in the area for some time, so the man may have got to know him before the events recorded here.

In the passage on the calling of Matthew (Luke 5:27–32) the significance of his calling a tax-collector is quite clear. Tax-gatherers were men who worked for the Roman Government, collecting taxes for the occupying forces by whatever means they could. This meant that most Jews regarded them as traitors, and would have nothing to do with them. They broke the ritual laws of purification by spending so much time with Gentiles (non-Jews). Jesus, by choosing one of these men for his friend, showed that he was not bound by society's conventions, but that his love reached out to everyone.

CLASS PREPARATION

We all need friends. Children make and break friendships quite quickly. Discuss with the children why they have friends and what they do with them. Encourage them to see that friends have mutual interests. They like being in each other's company. Friends talk, work, play, and share together. A true friend is always ready to help. All these aspects can be elaborated and developed in written and art work. Each child could write about 'my best friend'.

Ask the children if they can remember what it was like on their first day at school. Did they feel lonely, even though they were with a lot of other children? Perhaps they suddenly caught sight of someone they knew. What difference did it make? Poems or stories could be written to illustrate this change. Look up the story of Jesus and the blind man in John chapter 9. What difference did Jesus' friendship make in this man's life?

Ask, 'Are all your friends exactly like you?' After a moment's thought your children will realise that their friends are all very different. They could be encouraged to write about this. Jesus' friends were also very different in personality, behaviour and background. Think of Peter (Matthew 16:13–19; 26:31–35, 69–75; 14:25–32; John 21:1–19), Matthew (Matthew 9:9–12) and Thomas (John 11:16; 20:24–29). Other examples include Mary Magdalene (Luke 8:1–3), Zacchaeus (Luke 19:1–10), the woman of Samaria (John 4:7–42) and Nicodemus (John 3:1–12).

Children need to be taught that excluding others from their friendship can be hurtful. At the same time they need to know that they have to be careful who they have as their close friends. The parable of The Prodigal Son makes this point clear (Luke 15:11–13).

Participants: *Acting:* Jesus, Matthew, Pharisee, Simon, John, James, Andrew, Joshua, Benjamin, Eli, 3 or 4 others, Zebedee.
4 children with written work or pictures
4 children with prayers

PRESENTATION

Hymn: 'Peter's brown boat' (Come and Sing 27)

When Jesus was here on earth he had lots of friends. He chose twelve men to be his special friends. They left their jobs and worked with Jesus, helping him heal and teach. They spent a lot of time with him. We are going to tell you about how some of them came to be his friends.

Scene 1

Matthew   My name is Matthew. I am a tax-collector. I work for the Romans, collecting money from the people to pay their taxes. That is why most people don't like me. But Jesus is different. He wanted to be my friend. I am giving a party for Jesus so that my friends can get to know him too. Here they come now.

(*He introduces his friends to Jesus one at a time*)

Jesus, I'd like you to meet my friend Eli. He's a tax-gatherer too. . . And this is Joshua. . .and this is Benjamin. He works for the Romans too. Friends. I'd like you to meet Jesus.

(*All this action should be imagined to take place on the street outside Matthew's house. A passing Pharisee stops and stares.*)

Pharisee   Why do you want to meet these people? Don't you know they're all tax-collectors and bad people? They work for the Romans.

Jesus   I did not come to invite the good people to change their ways, but the bad ones. (*To Matthew*) Come on

Matthew, I'm waiting to share that meal with all of you. . . .

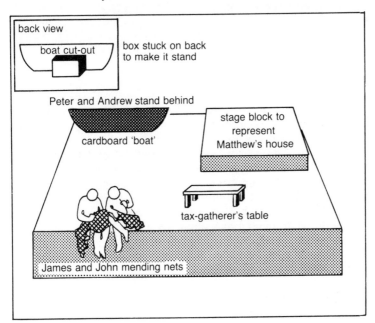

Scene 2

Simon   We must get on with mending these nets, Andrew. We'll need to go out in the boat in a few minutes.

Andrew   Yes, we can't afford to lose the catch because of broken nets.

(Enter Jesus)

Jesus   Hello Simon, and Andrew. How is the fishing going?

Andrew   Not too bad. It depends on the weather and how much we catch.

Jesus   It's a good life, fishing. But if you follow me I will teach you to catch men.

Simon   I'll come.

Andrew   Me too.

(*They walk a little way, and come up to James, John and Zebedee.*)

Simon   There are James and John. They look as if they are having trouble with their nets too.

Jesus   I need them to be my friends and help with my work too. . .James and John, I have a job for you to do. . .Come and follow me. . .

(*James and John throw down their nets and say goodbye to Zebedee, then Jesus and the four friends walk off together talking.*)

This week we have been thinking about our friends. These children have written/drawn pictures about what they do with their friends. (*Three or four children*) So what do we do with our friends? We play with them, talk, go on visits, make things and share our books and toys with then.

These children have written prayers thanking God for their friends (*four children*).

Hymn: 'Jesus is the best friend' (Come and Sing 37)

FOLLOW UP

1 Expand on any of the ideas suggested in the 'Class Preparation Section' that particularly appealed to the children. In particular look up incidents in the lives of Jesus and his friends. Some of these are suggested in the 'Preparation' section. Others given here show the disciples in all sorts of different ways, sometimes agreeing, some-times arguing, sometimes doing things that please Jesus, and at other times being taught by him. They reveal the different moods and occupations that all groups of friends experience. The children could write, draw or mime these situations. Using several references about one person, they could collect the information from these to write a character study or poem about that person. They could also make up 'passports' of each of Jesus' friends, with a picture and details about them.

Matt. 8:23–27 – storm at sea
Matt. 10:1–15 – 12 disciples
Matt. 15:10–16 – explaining to friends
Matt. 16:13–28 – Peter
Matt. 17:1–20 - Transfiguration
Matt. 20:20–27 – James and John
Matt. 26:17–35 – Passover
Mark 9:33–36 – disciples arguing
John 1:35–50 – calling some friends

2 The children could make 'passports' of their own friends.
3 Using these references the children could make a book, entitled 'Things Jesus did with his friends', and a similar one for themselves.
4 Encourage discussion by asking questions such as: What is a good friend? Do we choose our friends?
5 Let the children write imaginatively about being one of Jesus' friends, using material from above.
6 Look up other Bible friends:
David and Jonathan 1 Sam. 18:1–4; 19:1–7,20; 2 Sam. 1:17–27. Paul and Timothy Acts 16:1; 1 and 2 Tim.; 1 Cor. 16:10; Phil. 2:19–23.

See also Outline 20 and Outline 35 on Jesus' friends.

14 Thank you

AIM

To show the importance of saying thank-you to God and to other people.

BIBLE BASE Luke 17:11–19

This story of Jesus healing ten men at once seems at first sight perhaps a little exaggerated. Ten men? However we must remember that people with infectious and incurable skin diseases, such as these were, were outcasts from the town and had no company except others in a similar condition. In Leviticus 13, in the Old Testament, the rules for treatment of such illnesses are clearly stated: 'A person who has a dreaded skin-disease must wear torn clothes, leave his hair uncombed, cover the lower part of his face and call out "Unclean, unclean". He remains unclean as long as he has the disease and he must live outside the camp away from the others.' Vv. 45, 46. Such people could not be reintegrated into society unless they had been declared clean by the priest.

The disease was not necessarily what we know as leprosy, but it was a fearful, disfiguring and ultimately a killer disease. Those who had it had no hope of a cure, except the miraculous.

In one sense all this makes it seem quite incredible that the men could forget to thank Jesus, but on the other hand it does remind us of the fundamental selfishness of mankind.

CLASS PREPARATION

Discuss with your class what it is like to be ill. You could make graphs of the incidence of the 'common childhood illnesses', and ask the children to describe in writing how they felt. If they were infectious and friends and brothers and sisters were kept away they will have some idea of how these men felt.

Talk about serious illnesses; ones people don't get better from. (Make sure you are not hurting any of your children; some may know people in this situation.) These days a lot can be done to help such people, using modern drugs and skills. Not so long ago there was very little that could be done. Discuss leprosy in the Bible and how the sufferers were treated. How would this feel? Explain to the children the reason for going to the priest. Tell the story of Luke 17:11–19. Explain why it was so unexpected that the one man who said 'thank you' was a Samaritan.

Ask the children to think about saying 'thank you'. How do they think Jesus felt when only one man came back to thank him? Have they ever had this kind of experience? Do they ever forget to say thank you; to friends, to Mum, to God? Write 'thank you' prayers and poems for use in the assembly.

Participants: *Acting* – Narrator, 10 leprosy sufferers, Introducer, 3 boys, 2 dinner ladies, girl, Jesus, (optional 'crowd'), 4 or 5 children to read prayers. You may prefer not to have both sets on stage at the same time. If so, you will need extra children as scene shifters.

PRESENTATION

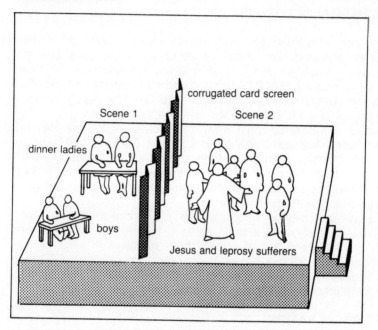

Introducer	Hello everyone. Our assembly today is about – well see if you can decide for yourselves. First we'll sing a hymn that might give you a clue.
Hymn:	'Thank you' (Sing to God 151)

Scene 1 (Dinner time at school)

Boy 1	Hey, this dinner is really nice today, isn't it?
Boy 2	Yes it is. I'd like some more, wouldn't you?
Dinner lady 1	Who would like seconds of the roast beef and Yorkshire pudding?
Boys	Me! Me! (*Hands wave in the air.*)
Dinner lady 1	Right, up you go, then.
Dinner lady 2	Here you are boys. A lovely large second helping for both of you.
Boys	Great!

Dinner lady 2	Haven't you forgotten something?
Whole class	Thank you.
Boy 3	Oooh, that apple you're eating looks nice. Can I have a bite?
Girl	Well. . .oh, go on then.
Boy 3	Mmmm. . .that's beautiful.
Girl	Haven't you forgotten something?
Boy 3	No, I don't think so.
Whole Class	Thank you.
Introducer	Well, these scenes may have been funny but the boys forgot to say two very important words, didn't they?
Whole class	Thank you.
Narrator	In the Bible we read a story about some people who forgot to say thank you. In a certain village there were ten men who suffered from leprosy.

(*Enter 10 leprosy sufferers, dressed in tatty clothes, some ringing bells.*)

They weren't allowed to mix with other villagers as it is a very infectious disease. They had to ring bells to warn people to keep away from them. One day the men heard that Jesus was coming. They stood a long way away from him and called:

(*Jesus enters opposite the men.*)

Leprosy sufferers	Jesus, Master, help us!
Jesus	Go and show yourselves to the priests.
Narrator	Then as the men went they found that they were indeed quite well again.

(*Men leap about rejoicing.*)

But one of the men turned back and fell at the feet of Jesus.

Leprosy sufferer	Oh Jesus, how can I ever thank you for all you've done for me!
Jesus	I'm glad you returned to thank me, but where are the other men I healed?

(*Jesus and the man go off talking together.*)

Narrator	Jesus loves us to say thank you to him. In the Bible we read, 'In the name of our Lord Jesus Christ always give thanks for everything to God the Father.'
Introducer	In class we've found lots of things we really want to thank God for.

Children read or recite prayers they have written themselves on this theme.

Hymn: 'If I were a butterfly' (Sound of Living Waters 106)

FOLLOW UP

1 Write 'before and after' poems for the leprosy sufferers.
2 Look up other healing miracles of Jesus'. Did people say thank you in these?
  Matthew 8:2,3 – Leprosy sufferer
  Matthew 9:2–6 – Paralysed man
  Matthew 12:10–13 – Paralysed hand
  Matthew 17:14–18 – Epileptic boy
  Mark 7:31–37 – Deaf-mute
  Luke 14:1–4 – Sick man
  John 4:46–54 – Official's son
  John 5:1–9 – Healing at the Pool
3 Make a 'thank you' montage of things we tend to take for granted such as sunshine, water, homes, etc.
4 Make 'thank you' posters to hang in strategic points around the school – over the serving hatch, in the library, etc.
5 Could a nurse or doctor give a short talk on modern ways of helping people cope with illness? Are there any local people who are ill who could be visited or written to, or have a tape-recorded message?

Other miracles of Jesus are in Outlines 15, 16, 17, 19.

15 Sharing

AIM

To show that it is good to share what we have with others.

BIBLE BASE John 6:1–13 – The Feeding of the Five Thousand.

This story comes just before Jesus' statement that he is 'the bread of life'. While with older children you might want to explore more fully that Jesus was saying that he was as important to our spiritual life as bread is to our physical life, younger children will enjoy the story as an example of the rewards of generosity.

The loaves mentioned were probably little flat cakes of bread, rather like baps. The fish would probably have been dried or pickled. It is important to make sure the children realise that what the lad gave to Jesus was just a typical picnic lunch.

CLASS PREPARATION

What kind of food do you like eating best? A great deal of work could flow from this discussion. Graphs could be made depicting favourite foods. Children could make giant 'plates' and fill them with pictures of their favourite meals.

Lead on to talk about bread. When do we eat bread? How do we eat bread? (toasted, etc.) Where do we eat bread? (picnics, packed lunches, etc.) Bread has always been one of man's staple foods.

The Bible is a practical book and clearly recognises man's pre-occupation with his basic needs. God meets man's needs – sometimes in spectacular ways. God promised Noah that the cycle of agricultural and seasonal events would continue 'while the earth remains' (Genesis 8:22). The children of Israel ate manna and quails in the wilderness (Exodus 16). God provided for Elijah and the widow of Zarephath (1 Kings 17:1–16).

The story of the boy with the five loaves and two fishes shows the power of God at work in the person of Christ. He took the little food the boy gave and made it more than enough for a vast crowd. Ask the children, 'What would you have done if you had been that boy?' He might have kept it for himself – or he might have been afraid of ridicule for offering so little. Instead, he gave what he had and shared in a miracle.

Any piece of sharing we do might seem small. Yet it could make a vital difference to someone.

Encourage the children to think and write about occasions when they have helped someone by sharing. Some children could make pictures to show how they could help in various situations.

Participants: *Acting* – John, Timothy, Jesus, Andrew, Mark, Mum, Disciples, Crowd.
    3 Children with writing
    3 Children with pictures

PRESENTATION

Props: Five baps and two fishes (cut out of paper).

Hymn: 'Who can, what can?' (Sing to God 128)

This week we have been thinking about sharing. These children have written about how they helped someone by sharing.
(*Three children*)
These children have made pictures about how they could help by sharing.
(*Three children*)
This is a story about a boy who helped Jesus by sharing.
Staging – Scene 1 – on stage

John	Have you heard? Jesus is by Lake Galilee.
Timothy	Let's go and see him.
Mark	I'd better ask my mum.

Scene 2 – off stage but in front of audience.
(*The three boys go 'off' amongst the rest of the school and John and Timothy say their lines from amongst the audience. Meanwhile Jesus and disciples come on stage so Timothy can point.*)

Mark	Can I go and see Jesus?
Mum	Whatever for?
Mark	Everyone is talking about him. I do want to see him for myself.
Mum	All right. I'll pack you some dinner . . . here you are, five little loaves and two small fishes.

Scene 3 – The boys arrive on stage to talk to Andrew.

John	What a crowd! Where is Jesus?
Timothy	There he is . . . with some of his special friends.
Mark	They look a bit worried. . . . Please tell us if we can help.
Andrew	Everyone is very hungry and there is no food.
Mark	My mum gave me some dinner. Five loaves and two little fishes – you can have them, if you like.
Andrew	Thank you. I will take them to Jesus.

Andrew took the food and brought it to Jesus. Jesus made it enough for all, with plenty to spare.

Prayer: Thank you, Lord Jesus, for everything you give us: for our homes, our parents, and our friends. Help us to share the good things we have with others. Amen.

    Please Lord, forgive us when we have been selfish: when we have wanted to keep everything and share nothing. Teach us to help to meet the needs of others. Amen.

Hymn: 'All that I have' (Sing to God 133)

FOLLOW-UP

1 Expand the ideas in the preparation section to include such things as maths work on foods (favourites, amounts eaten, etc.), and such activities as bread-making.
2 Read the Bible stories mentioned in the preparation.
3 Ask the children to illustrate the story. It would make a nice frieze.
4 Make a book of the stories in the Class Preparation section, entitled 'God feeds his people'.
5 Discuss fishing in the Sea of Galilee.

16 Hands

AIM

To get the children thinking about using their hands constructively to create and help.

BIBLE BASE Mark 5:21–43

The story of the healing of Jairus' daughter is interwoven with that of the woman who touched Jesus' cloak. In the two incidents described, hands play a part. The woman reached out in desperation and touched the cloak of Jesus. Jesus reached out in love to bring Jairus' daughter back to life. In the presentation we shall concentrate on the story of Jairus' daughter.

Jairus was an important person, but he was willing to be completely humble before Jesus in order to get his child made well again. Probably he had already tried the doctors and now felt that Jesus was his only hope.

The crying and confusion in verse 38 was the custom when a death had occurred, as it still is in many Eastern countries today.

CLASS PREPARATION

Introduce thinking about hands to your class by asking the children to make shapes with their hands. Experiment for a few minutes. Then ask them to make different noises using their hands. Clapping is an obvious one, but are there other ways? Give the children time to create something using their hands: modelling, sewing, drawing, baking, etc. Let them make suggestions and then choose, and give them plenty of time to complete their chosen creation. Perhaps these could then be put on display for the assembly.

Look through the assembly 'presentation' section and make sure all the ideas there are covered in class work in advance. Probably the whole class will enjoy making the puppets; in which case let them choose those for performance. Make sure you have plenty of time to make the puppets.

Encourage the class to think about how they can use their hands to help: washing up, dusting, cleaning shoes, etc. How they can use their hands to show love: stroking, shaking hands, cuddling, etc. Let them write poems and prayers to read in the assembly about the ways they use their hands.

Participants: *Acting* – 2 children demonstrating unkind hands, 'Policeman', Jesus, Jairus, servant, child, women, crowd.

Children to do 'hand dances', puppeteers, musicians, 3 children to read prayers.

Props: Policeman's helmet, puppets, musical instruments.

PRESENTATION

Hymn: 'Jesus' hands were kind hands' (Someone's singing Lord 33)

Introduction:
We use our hands for many different things. Our class has been thinking about some of the ways we use them.
(*Two children stand out at the front.*)
'Hands can be kind; an outstretched hand is kind. When we shake someone's hand it is a kind gesture (*children demonstrate*). Hands can also be unkind. They can smack, and point. A clenched fist is an unkind hand (*demonstrations*).

Our hands can speak for us too. A car driver knows whether to stop or go by looking at a policeman's hands (*demonstrate*).

Some people's hands can dance too. Some of us have made up hand dances to show you (*demonstrate.*)

We all use our hands to write and draw and cut out with. Our class has made these string puppets; we use our hands to pull the string and make the puppets move.

We made glove puppets too; we use our fingers to make the puppets' hands move.

We painted pictures using our fingers instead of a paint brush.

We have written a musical piece using our recorders and percussion instruments. We couldn't play it to you without using our hands.

We can clean shoes, dust, wash up, mend things, cook for others and use our hands to help other people.

There is a story in the Bible about a time when Jesus used his hands. We sang about Jesus' kind hands in our hymn. Now watch as the children act the story for you.

Scene 1 Crowd of children talking about Jesus, and how he healed people. They see Jesus coming and go to see him. Jesus moves amongst the crowd, talking to one and another.

Scene 2 Jairus forces his way through the crowd to Jesus, looking very worried, 'My daughter is very ill. Please will you come and make her better.'

Scene 3 Jesus and Jairus walk together, crowd following.

Scene 4 Servant rushes up. 'Don't bother the Teacher any longer. Your daugher has died.' Jesus turns to Jairus, 'Don't be afraid. Only believe.' Jesus turns to crowd and shows with his hand that they are to stay there. He and Jairus go to 'house'.

Scene 5 Inside house, group of women weeping and wailing. (*These could be in place ready at the start of the acting, and it would be more effective if the two halves of the story could be on two levels, with the house scene higher.*) Jesus goes in and sends them out. 'She is not dead, she is only sleeping.'

Scene 6 Jesus takes the child's hand and lifts her up. She smiles at Jesus. Mother and father look very happy.

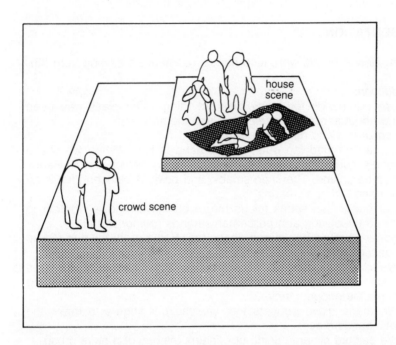

Prayer: Jesus always used his hands to help people and to make them happy. We have written some prayers and poems about the ways we use our hands to help others. (*Three or four children.*)

Hymn: 'He's got the whole world in his hands' (Sing to God 4)
We are going to use our hands to make actions about the song as we sing it. The song means that God is in control of the whole world – he looks after it lovingly, so it is as if he holds it in his hands keeping it safe.

FOLLOW UP

1 Go over any suggestions from the preparation section which were not fully covered, and anything that the children would like to expand from the presentation.
2 Let the children write stories about 'helping hands'.
3 Look up other Bible stories where hands were used to help.
   Luke 5:12–16 – Healing a leper
   Matthew 8:14, 15 – Healing Peter's mother
   John 12:1–8 – Mary anoints Jesus' feet
   John 13:3–12 – Jesus washes the disciples' feet
4 Look up and illustrate biblical uses of hands: for prayer, praise, etc. The children could create a series of pictures entitled 'Hands for

Worship'.

> Psalm 47:1 – clapping
> Psalm 134:2 – raised in prayer
> Psalm 150 – music and dancing.

5 Compare different people's hands: a very old person's, a baby's, a child's, etc. The children could try to describe these in writing.

6 Think about other parts of the body. Can any others be used in a helping way? If so, which?

17 Jesus heals a blind man

AIM

To show that, like Jesus, we should care for all kinds of people, even those whom others ignore.

BIBLE BASE Luke 18:35–43

This passage shows Jesus' love in action, reaching a man who was ignored by most of society. The most they would do would be to throw him a few coins to salve their consciences. He would have been a beggar simply because with his handicap he could not work, and there was no alternative.

CLASS PREPARATION

Ask the children to shut their eyes for a few minutes and imagine what it would be like to be blind. You could set simple tasks to do, ones they could do easily with their eyes open, but which are much more difficult with their eyes shut.

For example they could be asked to cross the room and open the door, find their reading books and open them, write their names, draw a picture of their house, put their coats on. . . . Let them write about the things they would miss if they were blind.

Explain that in Jesus' time the blind, the lame, etc. were the outcasts of society; the people who could not support themselves and who had to rely on help from other people in order to live. Talk about the people who are in need today. Explain that Jesus really cared about this man, whereas other people thought he was just being a nuisance. As followers of Jesus we should care for those who are left out and unwanted.

Let the children look up the stories of other 'down and outs' that Jesus helped, or read or tell the stories. They will then need to paint large pictures of these people, and prepare their explanations of what Jesus did for them for reading in the assembly. Suggested characters are:

Zacchaeus (outcast because he worked for the Romans) Luke 19:1–9
Samaritan woman (member of a despised race) John 4:5–41
Lepers – Luke 17:11–19
Matthew (tax gatherer – like Zacchaeus) Luke 5:27–31

Participants *Acting* – Blind man, Jesus, narrator, crowd
Musicians
Children with paintings and writing
Children with prayers.

PRESENTATION

Hymn: 'Look out for loneliness' (Someone's Singing Lord 36)

Today we are thinking about the way Jesus cared for people. We have drawn and painted pictures of some of the people Jesus helped. (*Let a few children hold up their pictures of people Jesus helped, from the list given in the preparation section, and explain briefly that in each case these were people who were not generally liked by the 'respectable' members of society.*)

Each of these people needed Jesus to care for them in a special way because nobody else did. We are going to act a play for you now, about another person whom Jesus helped.

(*It is suggested that music is used at certain points in the outline but this can be omitted.*)

Narrator   In Jericho there lived a blind man, who earned his food by begging at the entrance to the city.(*Music representing a blind man tapping with a stick and stumbling along. The blind man enters, mimes finding his way to his usual place and sits down, holding out his hands as if begging,*)

Narrator   He relied on what people put in his begging bowl in order to be able to buy food.

(*Busy music again. Crowd come together and look this way and then that as if searching for someone. Jesus could enter from the rear of the hall and make his way through the audience.*)

Blind man   What's happening? Who is it?

Crowd   Ssh. It's Jesus of Nazareth. He's coming this way. (*And so on*)

Blind man   Jesus of Nazareth? He could help me. (*shouts*) Jesus, Son of David, have pity on me!
Jesus, Son of David, have pity on me!

Crowd   Sshhh! Be quiet! He doesn't want to see you, you old fool. Be quiet, you dirty old beggar! (*And so on*)

(*The crowd mimes turning on the blind man, shaking their fists, shouting, shaking him.*)

Blind man   (*louder*) Jesus, Son of David have pity on me! Please listen to me. . . .

(*He stands up and waves his hands in the air in his effort to be seen. Jesus stops and looks around, slowly. When he sees the blind man he smiles, and points to him.*)

Jesus   There he is! Bring him to me, please.

(*Music again. The person nearest Jesus nudges his neighbour and points. This is repeated until one of those standing near the blind man leads him to Jesus. The crowd make a pathway through and all try to see what is happening.*)

Jesus   What do you want me to do for you?

Blind man   (*falling on his knees*) Sir, I want to see again.

Jesus   (*stoops down and touches him*) Then, see! Your faith has made you well.

(*The man stands up slowly, rubs his eyes, and turns slowly round, looking and pointing at things and people. This could all be accompanied by appropriate music. Then he bursts into life, running and jumping, flinging his hands about. The crowd begins to dance too, and the whole play ends with them all dancing round, looking joyful.*)

Narrator   The man who had been blind followed Jesus on his way, thanking him, and praising God that he could see again.

(*This gives an opportunity for the actors to leave the stage. They can file off, led by Jesus and the blind man.*)

When Jesus was on earth, he looked after a lot of people that most people couldn't be bothered with. If we are trying to live as his followers he expects us to do the same. Do we?

Prayer:
Prayers written by the children about looking after and helping people.

Hymns: 'Lord of the Loving Heart' (Sing to God 122)
'Mine are the hands to do the work' (Sing to God 134)
'Jesus' hands were kind hands' (Someone's Singing Lord 33)

FOLLOW UP

1 The children could find out something about Christians in history who have followed Jesus by helping those who were looked down upon by others: St Francis of Assisi, Dr Barnardo, Elizabeth Fry, etc. They could write about these people, imagining themselves to be one of those who were helped.

2 Use the people and incidents described in the assembly to compile a book 'Jesus helps the outcasts'.

3 Find out about areas of need in the world today. Is there anything practical the children can do to help those in need around the school?

4 Find out other times when Jesus gave sight back to blind people.
Matthew 9:27–31 – two blind men
Matthew 12:22 – man blind, dumb and possessed
Mark 8:22–26 – blind man at Bethsaida
John 9 – man born blind

See other outlines in this section for more miracles of Jesus.

18 The widow's coins

AIM

To encourage the children to be generous.

BIBLE BASE Luke 21:1–4

This story shows that God is concerned with our motives, not just our actions. The widow gave because she wanted to, and it was a sacrifice for her to do so. Children should be encouraged to give generously, and not for reward or praise. Look up Jesus' teaching on the subject of generosity (Matthew 6:1–4, 19–21, 24–34).

CLASS PREPARATION

Look at the parable of the tax-gatherer and the Pharisee (Luke 18:10–14) and talk about the likenesses between this parable and the story in Luke 21:1–4. Tell the children about the way of giving money in the Temple – open box, etc. Tell the children about 'Lord Smyth' who gave £1000 to the Children's Home, £1000 to the Nantwich General Hospital and £1000 to the Old People's Home. Can the children give you a word to describe this sort of person? Generous. Does being generous always mean giving large amounts like this? Ask for their reasons for their answers to this question. Read the story of Luke 21:1–4.

Participants: *Acting* – Leader, Reuben, Caleb, Asher, Benjamin, Andrew, James, Philip, Judas, John, Jesus.
　　Choral speaking – 3 groups of not less than 3 children each.

PRESENTATION

Hymn: 'All that I have' (Sing to God 133)
That hymn was about giving. That is the theme for our assembly today.

Props: Large box for offerings, silver coins, two copper coins.

Leader	One day Jesus and his friends were standing near the entrance to the Temple, where people made their offerings before going in to worship.
Reuben	I've had a good week. I doubled what I gained last week.

(*He drops a large amount of silver in the box.*)

Caleb	I sold a piece of poor land at a good price. I could never grow anything on it. Jotham wants to build a house there.

(*He drops in more silver.*)

Asher   Yes, I know. He's asked me to build it for him, and he's paying well. I can spare quite a lot this week.

(*Drops in silver*)

Benjamin   My crops have been abundant this year. With the market price so high, I've made a small fortune.

(*Flourishes a lot of silver*)

(*They go in*)

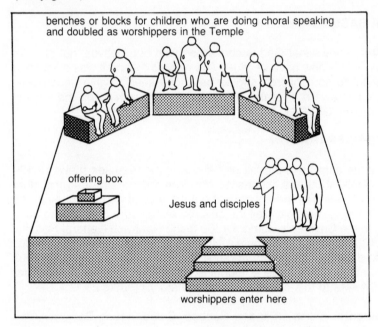

benches or blocks for children who are doing choral speaking and doubled as worshippers in the Temple

offering box

Jesus and disciples

worshippers enter here

Andrew   It must be very pleasant to be wealthy and able to give a lot.

James   They look well fed – they can well afford it.

Philip   I know the last man. He's really very generous.

Judas   It's all right being generous if you've no one to leave it to. He has no sons, he's unmarried.

John   But Andrew's right, isn't he, Master? They don't *have* to give as much as that, and they probably enjoy putting it in.

Jesus   Indeed, God loves a cheerful giver.

Philip   Oh, look at that poor woman in rags.

James   She's actually putting something in – oh, it's only two halfpennies.

Judas   It will make for awkward bookkeeping, those two tiny coppers among all the silver.

Andrew   She looks as though she needs it badly herself.

John   Perhaps she *wanted* to give something.

Jesus   I tell you, that poor woman has given more than all

those rich men put together. For they only gave what they could easily spare, while she gave all she had.
(*He and his friends go off.*)

Why do you think that Jesus said the poor widow had given more than all the rich people? Who do you think gave most?

Paul, who was one of the followers of Jesus, wrote these words about giving, in the Bible.

Choral speech: 2 Corinthians 9:7–11
Three small groups of children.

Group 1   Each one should give then, as he has decided. . . .
Group 2   not with regret. . . .
Group 3   or out of a sense of duty;
All   for God loves the one who gives gladly.
Group 2   And God is able to give you more than you need, so that you will always have all you need for yourselves and more than enough for every good cause. As the Scripture says:
Group 3   He gives generously to the needy; his kindness lasts for ever.

This passage says God will always give us all we need . . . not want. How much do we really need? . . . could we do with less than we have? . . . how much of what we have, could we give away and do without?. . .

Prayers:
Lord God, we want to thank you that you have given us so much and that you promise to give us what we need. Please help us not to be selfish, and to remember that our possessions are a gift from you.
Children's prayers about giving.

Hymn: 'The wise may bring their learning' (Sing to God 135)

FOLLOW UP

1 Ask the children to try to be honest with themselves about their motives for doing things.
2 Could you as a class do something sacrificial; such as giving up one week's pocket money for a charity? This would help the children to appreciate how the widow felt, and why Jesus praised her.
3 Let the children imagine the widow's feelings in the Temple when she saw all the money being given. Can they write about this?

Other assemblies on this theme are in outlines 10 and 15.

19 The paralysed man

AIM

To show Jesus as someone who can change lives.

BIBLE BASE Luke 5:17–26

The children will need to know that houses in Bible times were different from the houses they live in, so it was possible to climb on to the roof and make a hole in it.

The Pharisees were cross with Jesus because by telling the man that his sins were forgiven he was claiming that he could do what only God could do. They thought he was committing blasphemy. They were even more cross when the fact that the man was healed showed that Jesus had been justified in what he said.

CLASS PREPARATION

Show a picture of the paralysed man – explaining that he cannot move, and has to spend his time lying on a mattress. Ask the children how they think he feels. What would he do all day? How does he stop himself being bored? They could write about how they feel when they are ill and unable to go out, or perhaps some of them will have had broken limbs. How did they manage without an arm, or a leg?

Talk about times when a day has turned out completely different from what was expected. Perhaps a picnic was rained off, or a surprise trip to the sea-side was planned. How did they feel at the end of the day?

In this story about something that Jesus did, there was a man who could never have guessed how his day would end. Read the story.

Participants: *Acting* – Dan, Simeon, Ben, 2 Friends, 4 Pharisees, Peter, 3 Crowd and other Crowd, Narrator, Jesus.
Children with writing.
Children with prayers.

PRESENTATION

Hymn: 'Come let us remember' (Someone's Singing Lord 7)

These children are going to read about exciting days they have had (*3 children*).
Scene 1
Narrator   The man in our story today was not the sort of person

who ever did anything exciting. He was paralysed; he couldn't move, but just lay on his mattress day after day. As he lay there in his helpless state it was always a joy to him when someone called to see him. One day he was startled to see Dan and Ben. Dan asked a rather strange question.

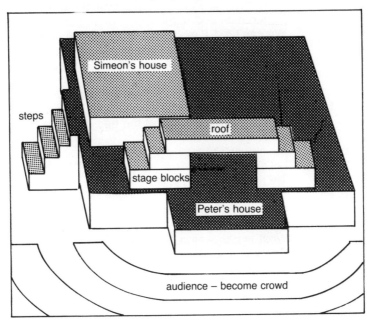

Make sure stage blocks are safe.
If you choose quite a small child for the part of the lame man, and strong boys for the friends, you could literally have the man lowered from the top of the stage block to the block below in a strong blanket. This would be lowered by its four corners. You may want to enlist the help of some of the biggest boys in the school to hold the upright stage block firm while this is going on.

Dan   Simeon, how would you like to walk again?
Simeon   What sort of a silly question is that? You know my legs are useless.
Dan   True, but we know someone who can help you: Jesus of Nazareth.
Ben   Jesus is a prophet and a great teacher and some people even believe he is the Son of God.
Dan   We believe he can heal you.
Simeon   That would be wonderful. But how can I get to him?
Dan   He is here in Capernaum. We will get some friends to help us carry you to him.
Simeon   Can he really make a paralysed man walk?
Ben   Yes, he has done many wonderful things. The sick are healed. The blind see again.

Simeon	Oh, but you say he is the Son of God?
Ben	Yes, that is what we believe.
Simeon	Then he could not care for the likes of me. There are lots of things I've done in my life that I'm ashamed of.
Ben	But Jesus cares for ordinary people like you and me.

Scene 2

Dan	That must be Peter's house over there with all those fishing nets and ropes drying on the steps.
Friend 1	We can't get Simeon through all those crowds.
Ben	Wait a minute . . . all those nets and ropes. And those steps at the side of the house – they lead to the roof. . . .
Friend 2	It would not be difficult to get the bed up onto the roof.
Friend 1	But how do we get it down through the flat roof?
Ben	Remove the tiles and let the bed down on the ropes. What do you think?
Simeon	I think you're crazy.
Dan	Let's try it.
Ben	Tie the ropes tightly, Dan.
Friend 2	The hole is almost wide enough.
Simeon	Can you see anything, Dan?
Dan	Yes Simeon, I can.
Friend 1	What is happening down there?
Simeon	Can you see Jesus?
Dan	Yes, he is just calming the crowd.
Ben	There's quite a lot of them down there.
Simeon	Dan, Dan, I don't think we should be doing this. I have no right to ask his help.
Dan	Maybe.
Ben	You just tell him of your need . . . ready.
Friend 2	Get a good grip on those ropes . . . steady. . . .
Simeon	Now wait fellows.
Ben	Save it till you can walk.
Dan	Stand by below! We are sending down a sick man.

Scene 3

Phar. 1	This looks like a bad case of paralysis.
Crowd 1	I say, Peter, do you often have people dropping in on you like this?
Crowd 2	They have a cheek doing this. . . .
Crowd 3	Look at this chap on the mat; he looks scared stiff.
Jesus	I say he is full of faith. My son, put away your fear. Your sins are forgiven.
Simeon	You know all about me . . . my shame . . . my guilt.
Jesus	You are forgiven.
Phar. 1	What sort of talk is this . . . it's blasphemy.
Phar. 2	Only God can forgive sins.
Phar. 3	Yes, indeed, to our God belong mercies and forgiveness.

Phar. 4	Who does this carpenter think he is?
Jesus	Why do you argue? Is it easier to say your sins are forgiven, or get up and walk?
Phar. 1	Well, anyone can say 'I forgive you', but you can't prove that God has forgiven him.
Jesus	That is true, of course. But so that you know I do have power on earth to forgive sins . . . I say to you, pick up your mat and walk, and go home.
Crowd 1	He's getting up.
Crowd 2	This is amazing.
Crowd 3	Where can a man get such power?
Phar. 2	There can be only one answer . . . the thought frightens me. Maybe what he says is true!
Peter	How do you feel, man?
Simeon	I've never felt better in all my life . . . has God ever done so much for a man as he has done for me today . . . he has given me new legs . . . and new life . . . Lord . . . Lord.
Narrator	There was no happier man in all Capernaum that day. The crowds were amazed . . . they looked up into a hole in the roof thanking God.

Jesus made that day quite exciting for the paralysed Simeon, didn't he? And the Pharisees found it was not what they had expected either.

Just think for a few minutes about how nice it is to have surprises . . . times when things don't happen as we expect . . . days that turn out different.

Prayer:
We have written prayers and poems about this.

Hymn: 'Stand up, clap hands' (Someone's Singing Lord 14)

FOLLOW UP

1 Let the children write 'exciting day' stories.
2 Look up other times when the Pharisees disapproved of what Jesus was doing, e.g. Luke 6:6–11, John 5:1–18, Mark 7:1–13.
3 Find out more about houses in Bible lands, and other lands. Why and how are they different from our houses? Can the children draw and make models? How about a Bible village?
4 Find out about how people lived when Jesus was alive (see resource section). What was different? After this the children can imagine what it was like and write about a day in the life of an Israelite child. They could also write about a day in their own lives and compare the two.

20 Working for Jesus

AIM

To show that Jesus cares and has power to heal; we too should care for the handicapped.

BIBLE BASE Acts 3:1–10

This is the first story recorded in detail after the gift of the Holy Spirit has turned the small group of frightened believers into people of bold faith. The early church met together in homes to worship Jesus but also continued to worship in the Temple. Peter and John were going to the Temple for a service at three o'clock in the afternoon. They were confronted with a man who was desperately in need of help. He received far more than he expected.

There were many beggars in Jerusalem in NT times, as those who could not work had no other way of getting money to live on. The lame, the blind, and those who were too sick to work would gather at the gates of the Temple in the hope that the worshippers would provide for their needs.

Peter was absolutely certain of Jesus' power to heal this man; he did not suggest that the man tried to get up – he commanded, with such authority and conviction that the man obeyed.

PREPARATION

Children are active individuals. Ask them what they like *doing* best at home and school. Can they imagine what it would be like not to use their legs? How do we use our legs here in the classroom? What games do we play in the playground? The children could list as many activities as they can think of which involve the use of their legs. These could be classified under various headings:- fun, work, leisure, games or helping. These could be illustrated – perhaps using simple 'pin men'. Children could write about how they use their legs at home, in the playground or the park.

Which of these activities would we miss most if we lost the use of our legs? Think of elderly bedridden people, and children and adults who spend their lives in wheel-chairs. How can we make their lives happier if we meet them?

The well known story of the paralysed man who was brought to Jesus by his four friends is worth telling again (Mark 2:1–12). Jesus cared for those who were handicapped. So should we.

Participants: *Acting* – Ben, Sam, Tim, Peter, John, other beggars,

worshippers.
    Children with writing.
    Children with pictures.
    Children with prayers.

PRESENTATION

Hymn: 'O Jesus we are well and strong' (Someone's Singing Lord 40)

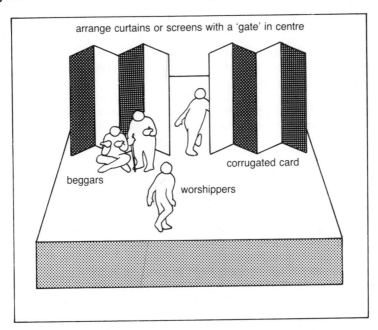

arrange curtains or screens with a 'gate' in centre

corrugated card

beggars

worshippers

At Whitsun we remember how the Holy Spirit was given to the first Christians, just as Jesus promised. Wonderful things began to happen. People's lives were changed. We are going to tell you about one of these people. At the beginning of our story he could not walk.

Ben   My name is Ben. I love walking, running and leaping. But there was a time when I could not do any of those things. You see, I was born a cripple. I will tell you what happened. We will pretend to go back to the time when I could not walk.

Ben   Ah! Here come my friends, Sam and Tim.

Sam, Tim   Are you ready, Ben? We will help you down to the Gate called Beautiful at the Temple.

Ben   You are very kind to do this for me every day. How I wish I could use my legs to work for my living. I hate having to beg for money.

(*Sam and Tim help Ben to his place by the Temple Gate*)

Ben   (*to people going into the Temple*) Will you spare something for a poor cripple? Ah! Here come two more,

perhaps they will be generous (*holding up his bowl*).
Will you have mercy on a poor cripple?

(*Peter and John stop and look at Ben*)

Peter   Look at us. I have no silver and gold, but I give you
what I have; in the name of Jesus Christ of Nazareth,
walk.

(*Peter takes hold of Ben by the right hand and lifts him to his feet*)

Ben   I can walk! I can run. . .and jump! Praise God!

Hymn: 'Silver and Gold have I none' (Sound of Living Waters 90)

We have been thinking about how we use our legs.
These children have drawn pictures. . .and these children have written
about how they use their legs.

Prayers: for children and adults in hospital and for those in wheel-
chairs, for God's help to use our legs to do his will.
(*use children's prayers*)

FOLLOW UP

1 Read Peter's own account of what happened and why, in Acts 3:11–
16. Let the children write about the man's feelings after the miracle
had happened. How do they think Peter felt? And what about the
passers-by? Perhaps their thoughts on the story could be recorded
on tape as a 'news bulletin'.
2 Look up Acts 5:12–16 for a brief account of more miracles. Could
the children expand these 'bare bones' into stories?
3 Encourage the children to think about how it feels to be handicapped
in some way. Discuss the state of handicapped people now and
compare it with the life of this man. Is there some practical way the
children could help local handicapped people?
4 Take the class for a walk round your local area imagining that they
are pushing a wheel-chair. See how difficult it would be and ask
them to make suggestions for how it could be improved.

Another healing of a lame man is in outline 19.

21 Living together

AIM

To consider the kind of people we need to be in order to live together happily.

BIBLE BASE Colossians 3:8–17

The letter to the church at Colosse, from which this passage is taken, was written by Paul to encourage and strengthen the Christians there. They were living in a pagan society, and Paul here stresses the change in their lives that they should work for as a result of becoming Christians. The main theme of this passage is that bad things should be replaced by good. Children usually accept that they are not perfect, and that things in themselves and their friends often spoil their friendship. They can be encouraged to fight the things in their own characters that they do not like.

CLASS PREPARATION

Ask the children to imagine that they are alone in the world, with no one else to see, touch or talk to. What would it be like? Let them record their ideas in writing.

Explain that this seems such a strange idea because people were made so that they need other people. In a perfect world we would all be happy together all the time. Is it like this? Why not? Discuss characteristics which spoil relationships. Often it is one particular thing that makes us dislike a person. If we are honest we have to admit that we all have some of these things wrong with us. Let the children think about this, but do not allow them to start criticising each other. A few minutes silence to think would be useful here.

These things are like dragons; they can eat up and destroy the good things. We need 'knights' to overcome these dragons. The knights are the good qualities, such as kindness, patience etc. Read the Colossians passage to the children and see if they can pick out the dragons and the knights.

Let them draw or make collage models of these dragons and knights for use in the assembly.

Participants: *Acting* – knights and dragons, suitably labelled. Paul, writing at a desk.

Speech – narrator,
Children with writing.

PRESENTATION

Hymn: 'Think, think on these things' (Someone's Singing Lord 38)

Prayer 'O Lord our God, you know what we are like inside, what we are thinking and what we want. Please take over our thinking and our wanting so that, forgetting about other things, we may want to think about you. In Christ's Name. Amen.'

Today we are thinking about how we can learn to live together with other people so that we do not argue or fight or break friends. First of all I want you to close your eyes and imagine that you are all alone; there is no one else anywhere.

Some children are going to read you their thoughts about what it would be like to be all alone (*three or four children read*).

It would be very strange, wouldn't it? That is because God made us to need other people. But as our prayer reminded us, we do not always live as he intended us to. Some people in the Bible had this problem too. A man called Paul wrote them a letter, encouraging them to try to be better. Listen to a part of it.

Read Colossians 3:8–17.

Divide the children into two groups: Knights and Dragons. Label each with one of the following names. Knights: Peace, Love, Gentleness, Patience, Kindness, Forgiveness, Truth. Dragons: Anger, Hate, Insult, Lying, Complaining, Swearing, Temper.

Child narrator points to the Dragons:

Narrator These are things in our lives which hurt other people and us too. They make us unloved. They get bigger and more powerful if we do not try to stop them.

Child points to the Knights:

Narrator These are the good things in our lives which can help us to fight the dragons. We thought these were like the knights who in the old stories went out to fight the dragons.

(*Let Knights and Dragons enact a fight*)

Narrator Fighting is hard work and we need help. God helps us to fight these things.

Hymn: 'When a knight won his spurs' (Someone's Singing Lord 34)

FOLLOW UP

1 Tell the legend of St George, and let the children illustrate it.
2 Study knights, armour and heraldry in more depth. Make models.
3 Look up the 'armour of God' in Ephesians 6.

SECTION 3: STORIES JESUS TOLD
22 What can I do?

AIM

To show the children that we all have gifts which we should use to the best of our ability to serve God and other people.

BIBLE BASE Matthew 25:14–30

The parable of the talents. In this parable the 'talents' seem to be some sort of money. The word is translated variously in different versions of the Bible. The New Bible Dictionary tells us, 'The talent was not a coin but a unit of monetary reckoning. Its value was always high, though it varied with the different metals involved and the different monetary standards.' From this parable the word has passed into modern speech to mean any natural gifts or abilities. The parable teaches that we all have different gifts and abilities, and God wants us to use them all for him and not to neglect them or hide them.

CLASS PREPARATION

Give each child a piece of paper and ask them to write down the thing they think they are best at. Explain that it can be anything, not just a school lesson, but something they do at home or some characteristic like helpfulness or kindness. Then ask them to write down something they would *like* to be good at. Tell them not to let anyone else see their paper. Let the children choose partners and ask each one to write down what he thinks his partner is best at. When they have all done this, let them compare what they have written and see if their friend agrees with them about what they can do best. Ask if they think the thing they *would like to be able to do* is better or more important than the thing they *can* do.

Discuss this and help them to see that we all have different gifts which are all equally important, and it is the way we use them that counts. Read or tell the story of the talents and explain that the man who had one talent was not punished because he had only one but because he did not use it.

Make puppets of master and three servants.

Props: coins and a spade.
The puppets should be as large as possible and their features should be very clearly marked.

Participants: 14 children to demonstrate things they are good at.

Actors or puppeteers – master, 3 servants. Children to read.

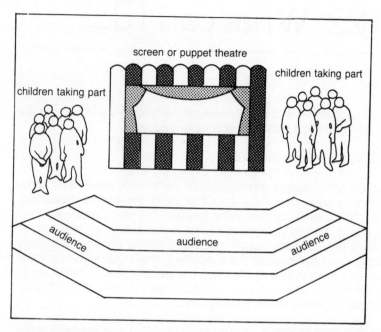

children taking part

screen or puppet theatre

children taking part

audience

audience

audience

PRESENTATION

Leader   We will sing 'Hands to work and feet to run' (Someone's Singing Lord 21).

While we are singing this, will you notice some of the things we all have which we can use to help one another.

What things did you notice?

(The answers should come back hands, feet, eyes, minds, hearts.)

We can all use these things in different ways.

(Let as many children as possible tell something which some people can do. They should rehearse this so that they speak out clearly and follow quickly one after the other. Alternatively it could be recorded on tape beforehand and played back at the assembly – most children like to hear their own voices on tape!)

Child 1   Some of us can use our hands to draw and paint well (*with objects as examples*)

Child 2   or our feet to run fast or jump high,

Child 3   some of us can use our voices to sing sweetly

Child 4   or to speak clearly

Child 5   some of us are good at games

Child 6   or maths

Child 7   others can write good stories

Child 8	some of us are quick to notice when people are in trouble and to help them
Child 9	some are generous and like to share things
Child 10	some can use their hands to knit and sew
Child 11	or make things from wood or clay
Child 12	some can bake and cook
Child 13	others can arrange flowers beautifully
Child 14	or play the piano or guitar or recorder.
Leader	God has given each one of us gifts, and he wants us to use them for him and to help other people. Jesus told a story about this.
	(Matthew 25:14–28 This story could be read while children use puppets to show the actions. It is suggested that a teacher does the reading, or that it is divided into sections for children to read. You might like to have different children reading the speech of each of the characters. Alternatively, children could mime the roles as the story is read.)
Leader	The master was angry with the third servant because he did not use the talent he was given. . .In the same way we can use, or waste our abilities.

Prayers: We thank you Heavenly Father, for all the things we are able to do. Please help us to please you by doing them well. Amen.
Dear Lord God, thank you for our hands and feet, our minds and our voices. Please help us to use them to help other people in as many ways as we can. Amen.

Leader	Let us sing 'Jesus' hands were kind hands' (Someone's Singing Lord 33).

FOLLOW UP

This assembly gives the opportunity to let children choose some piece of work which they would really like to do, e.g. cooking a special dish, artwork, lettering, writing stories, making models. Encourage them to keep at it until they have produced the very best of which they are capable. It might be possible to have a display of work which another class could be invited to come and see. Those who are good at games, PE, dancing, music, or reciting poetry could put on a demonstration. Why not invite some of the local elderly people to come and see it?

See outlines, 23, 24, 26, 27, 28, 29 for more stories Jesus told.

23 Choices

AIM

To try to enable children to make right choices. This assembly encourages us to base our choices upon the teachings of Jesus.

BIBLE BASE Matthew 7:24–27

At the beginning of Matthew chapter 5, Jesus gathered his disciples round him and began to teach them. The teaching continues right through to the end of chapter 7 and is known as the Sermon on the Mount. In it Jesus speaks of the Kingdom of Heaven and those who belong to it. He tells his followers how they ought to live and shows how the Old Testament law, and especially the Ten Commandments, can be applied to individual lives. He explains that he has come not to destroy the law but to fulfil it (Matthew 5:17) and he points out that the law applies not only to outward actions but to inward thoughts. So hatred is as bad as murder and coveting another man's wife as bad as adultery. The story of the two houses is told at the end of the sermon. It illustrates the wisdom of listening to the words of Jesus and obeying them.

CLASS PREPARATION

Tell a story of two children who find some money. One of them says, 'finders keepers'. The other says, 'We must take it to the police station.'

Ask the children if they ever have to make decisions like this and encourage them to give examples. Let them act out their ideas. Be ready with a few more ideas if they don't produce them, e.g. 1) Some children break something belonging to someone else. They must choose either to own up or to pretend they didn't do it.

2) As some children go past a supermarket they decide that they would like some sweets but none of them has any money. Shall they go home and get their pocket-money or go into the shop and take some sweets?

3) A new child comes to school looking very shy and lonely. She comes from another country or another region of this country and speaks differently from the other children in the school. Some of the children laugh and make fun of her because of this. Should we join in or should we try to make friends with her?

Jesus told a story about two men who had to make a choice. Read the story of the two houses from the Good News Bible or from a simple story book, e.g. Stories Jesus Told (Giraffe Books, published by Scripture Union).

Let groups of children make sound effects using percussion instruments to illustrate rock, sand, rain and wind, the fall of the house, e.g. the steady beat of a drum for rock, quick notes on a xylophone for sand, etc. Let the children give their own suggestions for suitable instruments. A music lesson could be used for this.

Participants: 2 children for playlet (or more according to what they suggest). Choral speaking: 13 children. Musicians.

PRESENTATION

Hymn:	'Father lead me day by day' (Sing to God 129)
Leader	Choices, choices, choices! We are always having to make them. Every day we must choose. Listen to some children making choices.

(*Two children walk on, talking as they come and looking into a purse. They stand mid-stage.*)

1st Child	There's a five pound note and two pounds in it.
2nd Child	And two 50p's.
1st Child	What should we do with it?
2nd Child	Perhaps we ought to take it to the police station.
1st Child	I don't see why we should. After all we found it and everyone says 'finders keepers'.
2nd Child	Yes, but it must belong to someone.
1st Child	Of course it does, but we don't know who. Anyway they should have been more careful.
2nd Child	Perhaps they really need the money.
1st Child	That's nothing to do with us. Just think what we can do with it. Come on let's go and spend it.
2nd Child	It seems almost like stealing to me.

(*They go off still arguing.*)

(*This is only a suggestion. It would be better to let the children use their own ideas and make up their own dialogue. If time permits two such conversations could be used.*)

Leader	Jesus told a story about two men who had to make a choice.
Reading:	(*Solo speaker, groups 1 (8 children) and 2 (4 children), musicians.*)
Solo	So then anyone who hears these words of mine and obeys them is like a wise man who built his house on rock.

(*Drum beat, or other 'rock' noise.*)

Group 1	The rain poured down. (*rain music*)
	The rivers overflowed (*river music*)
	And the wind blew hard against that house. (*wind music*)

Group 2	But it did not fall because it was built on rock.
Solo	But anyone who hears these words of mine and does not obey them is like a foolish man who built his house on sand.
(*sand music*)	
Group 1	The rain poured down. (*rain music*)
	The rivers overflowed. (*river music*)
	And the wind blew hard against that house. (*wind music*)
All	And it fell. (*cymbal or drum crash*)
Solo	And what a terrible fall that was. (*quietly*)
Leader	So the man who built his house on the rock is like the person who listens to the words of Jesus and follows in his ways. Let's now sing a song about choosing to follow Jesus – 'The journey of life' (Someone's Singing Lord 28).

Prayers: We ask, Lord, that we may make the right choices today. Show us the way you want us to live and help us to choose that way. Amen.

Dear Lord God, please help us to choose right and not wrong, to be kind rather than unkind, honest rather than dishonest, and always to follow you. Amen.

FOLLOW UP

1 Older groups could read the Ten Commandments, Exodus 20:1–17, and discuss how they apply to us today. Exodus 19 gives the immediate background to this. See also the 'Encyclopaedia of Bible Stories' (published by Scripture Union and recently reprinted under the title 'Book of Bible Stories in colour') pages 40–50.
2 Set up a display using children's illustrations with the theme: 'Which would you choose?' Suggestions are: house on sand, house on rock; tidy/untidy bedroom; regular meals, bowl of rice; bossy friend, helpful friend; wasting time, using time.

24 Keep on praying

AIM

To encourage the children to pray.

BIBLE BASE Luke 11:5–8

This story which Jesus told is an illustration of the fact that God does answer prayer and, even if it seems otherwise, we should keep on asking until we get an answer. Parents will often be influenced by the urgent pleading of a child, and God cares for us far more than a parent. There are many instances in the Bible of God's answers to prayer and many people today still experience God's care for mankind in his answers to prayer.

CLASS PREPARATION

A practical way of introducing this assembly to your class would be to make them 'badger' you for something. Perhaps you could hint that, 'We might go out to play rounders later on', and then say no more about it, except 'We'll see' until you have been asked a few times. After the game, ask the children why they think you gave in. Point out that children are usually quite good at getting adults to do something just by 'keeping on' at them, but sometimes adults use this as a way of seeing whether a child is really concerned about what he is asking for. If they had not really wanted to play rounders, they would not have kept on asking, and the game would have been forgotten. Jesus told a story which is a bit like this; he was trying to explain that God sometimes delays in answering our prayers.

Let the children paint pictures to accompany the poem.

Look at stories showing how God answers prayer, e.g. Elijah (1 Kings 18:16–46), Moses and the Red Sea, Brother Andrew (God's Smuggler), George Muller.

Participants: 4 children for playlets.
Group of children to read poem.
Groups of children to prepare and hold up pictures. The pictures shown here are suggestions which children could copy.

PRESENTATION

Useful Props: Newspaper, book.
We have been thinking about asking people for help. Sometimes we

go to our parents for help, like this.

John   Will you help me with my bicycle chain, Dad? It has come off.

Dad   (*reading paper*) Not now, I'm busy. I'll do it later.

John   Please, Dad, I want to go for a ride with my friends, now.

Dad   All right, I'll see what I can do.

Sometimes someone comes to us for help.

Jane   I can't tie my laces. Will you help me Susan?

Susan   I am just in the middle of this story. Come back when I've finished.

Jane   Please help me now. I want to go out to play.

Susan   All right, I will.

Sometimes we are rather slow to help others. But God is always ready to help us if we trust him, and keep on asking for his help.

Jesus told a story about a man who was slow to help his friend. The friend came to him at rather an unusual time. Listen to this poem and watch as we show you the pictures.

The Friend at Midnight

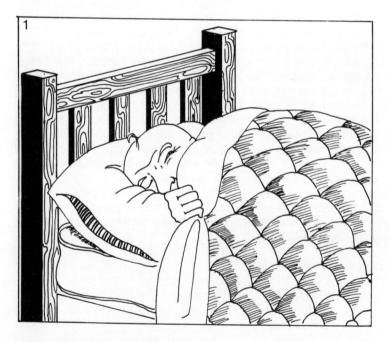

Who's that knocking at my door,
What can he have come for?
(He's still knocking, can't he wait?)
It's the middle of the night,
I'll have to rise and find a light.

Now, get the window open wide,
I'll see who's shouting outside.
'Whatever do you want with me?
You have woken me and my family.'

'Friend, a visitor has come,
I am feeling sad and glum.
My bread cupboard is quite bare.
Have you got three loaves to spare?'

'Some loaves? Only three you said,
I may be slow to leave my bed,
But I will help you in your need,
Your friend shall have a mighty feed.'

The friend in this story helped because he realised the man was really in need. Sometimes we expect God to answer our prayers the minute we ask him, but often we have to wait for an answer. But he always gives us what we need. He knows that better than we do. Let's pray about this now.

Prayer: Dear Father God, thank you that you want us to talk to you. Please help us to remember that you want us to keep on asking you about things, even if we don't get an answer straight away. Help us to trust you, and learn that you will always answer us. Amen.

Hymn: 'What a friend we have in Jesus' (Golden Bells 64)

FOLLOW UP

Talk about things the children really want; it might be a possession, or an attribute, such as ability to control temper, or a skill, or it might be something they want for someone else, a sick friend for example. Let them write individual prayers to take home and use.

Jesus told his friends some other stories about praying. Look these up and make a book, 'Jesus teaches about praying'.

Luke 18:10–14 – Pharisee and tax collector
Matthew 6:5–14 – How to pray

Discuss with the children when 'keeping on' at parents or teacher is a bad thing.

See outline 25 for another assembly on prayer.

25 The Lord's Prayer

AIM

To help children's understanding of what prayer is, using the words of the Lord's Prayer.

BIBLE BASE Luke 11:1–4

The Lord's Prayer is still used quite frequently in many different situations, so even if you do not use it regularly in school, the children are likely to meet it from time to time. It is a 'sample' prayer giving various aspects of prayer in a sort of summary – those things relating to God, and then requests relating to men.

Prayer is talking to God and the children need to be aware of the fact that God is holy and should be approached with respect; yet at the same time he is ready to listen to any sincere prayer.

NB This is not a 'story' Jesus told, but a very important part of his teaching.

CLASS PREPARATION

Find out if the children know the words of the Lord's Prayer by heart, and what they think it means. Discuss their ideas. Talk about prayer in general. What do they think it is? Do they pray? Who are they praying to?

Talk about the need to be sincere. Why should we mean what we say? Can the children think of any times when it would be very important to be sincere? Point out that relationships between people are better when they can rely on and trust one another. In our relationship with God, we should try always to mean what we say.

Participants: Acting – a) 2 children 'praying'.
b) 7 speakers + group of actors for 'how to pray'.
c) Housewife, vicar, man with dog, child, teacher.
7 readers + rest of class for the 'Lord's Prayer'.

PRESENTATION

Hymn: 'Our Father' (Sing to God 146)

Narrator   Today we are going to think about prayers, and in particular the Lord's Prayer. Some people say their

	prayers like this.
First Child	(*Kneeling in attitude of prayer with clenched hands, tightly closed eyes and upturned face.*)
	Dear God, please give me a bike for my birthday, and a Cindy doll with a complete wardrobe and a new dress and a pair of shoes, and please let me have a happy time at the party on Saturday and please let me win a prize. Oh yes, and please help me to pass my piano exam, even though I haven't practised properly. Please don't let Mary Jane be chosen for the netball team instead of me, and may Susan be away from school for the rest of the week because I am not friends with her any more. Amen.
Narrator	I don't really think that was the kind of prayer that God wants us to pray, do you? It was rather selfish. Jesus gave us the Lord's Prayer as a 'pattern' prayer to show us the sort of things we should ask God for. But some people pray that prayer like this.
Second child	(*Kneeling as did the first child, recites the Lord's prayer so fast that it becomes an indistinct gabble which ends in a very loud 'Amen'.*
Narrator	I don't think God wants us to pray like that either. People have all sorts of different ideas about the position you should be in when you pray.

(*Enter a small group of children, who do what the speakers say, and speakers.*)

Speaker 1	You must kneel down when you pray, and put your hands together.
Speaker 2	No, we always stand up to pray in our church.
Speaker 3	You get right down on the floor and bow your head down to touch the ground.
Speaker 4	You stand up and lift your hands above your head.
Speaker 5	Hands in front of you, you mean.
Speaker 6	You sit down to pray, of course.
Speaker 7	You kneel down and rest your elbows on a ledge. We do it that way in our church.

(*The speakers should try to say these lines as fast as possible so that the actors are no sooner in one position than they have to move.*)

Narrator	Do you really think it matters? I think the most important thing is that we should really be talking to God. Let's ask some people where they do their praying.

(*Enter a housewife (with duster), a vicar (with Bible), a man (with toy) dog, a child, and a teacher (with register).*

Housewife	I talk to God while I'm doing the dusting. It's a nice easy job I don't have to think about, so I can think about God instead.
Vicar	I pray in church, of course, but I also pray at home.
Man with dog	I pray while I'm walking the dog in the morning. It's

	nice and peaceful then.
Child	I pray at all sorts of times, like when I fall over, or get my sums wrong.
Teacher	I talk to God about my class.
Narrator	One prayer nearly everyone knows is the Lord's Prayer – the one Jesus taught his friends. We have been thinking about what the Lord's Prayer really means, and have added explaining bits of prayer in between the parts of the Lord's Prayer. We are going to say this prayer to you now. If you know the Lord's Prayer you could join in with us.

(*This part of the assembly will be most effective if the Reader passages are spoken by small groups of children, who have memorised them, and the actual words of the Lord's Prayer by the whole class. Arrange your Readers to look attractive, on blocks, standing and sitting. They do not need to close their eyes, as this will tend to make them speak more quietly, but they should try to remember that they are saying a prayer.*)

Reader 1	Maker of heaven and earth, Maker of all living things, Maker of men, The power and life of the universe, Beyond all space and time, And yet we can call you. . . .
All	Our Father who art in heaven.
Reader 2	Because you are holy, Because you are without sin, We stand in awe of you, and so we pray,
All	Hallowed be thy name.
Reader 3	You bring peace and love Into the hearts of men. May we work with you, our Father, To bring this peace and love into the world,
All	Thy kingdom come. Thy will be done on earth as it is in heaven.
Reader 4	You have made us and you love us. You give us all we need. Teach us to share with others what you give, So that we can pray. . . .
All	Give us this day our daily bread.
Reader 5	We know we do wrong, We need your forgiveness. Help us to forgive others too.
All	Forgive us our trespasses, as we forgive them that trespass against us.
Reader 6	Help us to stand up for what is right. We cannot manage without you, Father, so we pray. . . .
All	Lead us not into temptation, but deliver us from evil.

Reader 7   We know that you are great and wonderful,
              And that you will never change,
All   For thine is the kingdom, and the power and the glory.
              For ever and ever. Amen.

Hymn: 'Father hear the prayer we offer' (Sing to God 121)

FOLLOW UP

1 Think about other prayers that the children say regularly. What do they mean? (e.g. The Grace, the Magnificat (Luke 1))

2 Look up some of the prayers in the Bible. Discuss the different kinds of prayer they represent.
Exodus 33:12–23 – Moses speaks to God
1 Kings 8 – Solomon's prayer at the Dedication of the Temple
Psalms – many different prayers
John 17 – Jesus prays for his followers

3 Look up some of the answers to prayers in the Bible, e.g. Hannah (1 Samuel 1), Samuel (1 Samuel 3), Elijah (1 Kings 18).
Talk about answers to prayer in the lives of people such as George Muller.

4 Let the children write their own prayers for the next few assemblies, or use them in class at the end of the day.

5 Can they write any other 'paraphrases' for the Lord's Prayer, similar to the one used in the assembly?

6 Look up Jesus' teaching on prayer, in the Sermon on the Mount. Why do the children think he said what he did? (Matthew 6:5–15)

7 Make charts for different types of prayer using pictures cut out of magazines, catalogues, etc. to illustrate 'thank you', 'sorry', 'please' prayers.

26 Don't hold grudges

AIM

To show that forgiving each other and being forgiven is an important aspect of living together.

BIBLE BASE Matthew 18:21–35

This story that Jesus told is one that shows the importance of being prepared to forgive other people. Those who are unwilling to forgive may find that they in turn are not forgiven. The teaching here is closely connected with that given at the time of giving the 'Lord's Prayer'.

This story is told in answer to a question about forgiveness, when Peter, Jesus' friend, wanted to know how often he should forgive someone.

CLASS PREPARATION

Tell the story of two friends. One day Sarah accidentally broke her friend's recorder. Joanne was very keen on music and she was very upset when she saw a piece broken off her recorder. 'I hate you, Sarah', she cried, 'I'm never going to speak to you again. I shall never forgive you . . . never.' There were two very unhappy little girls who went home from school that night.

Ask the class, 'Do you think that Joanne kept her word? Did she talk to her friend again? What would you have done?' Ask if people usually stay cross for a very long time. Do their parents? What about their teacher? Is it a good idea to stay cross for days and to hold grudges? If not, why not? Explain that being bitter and unforgiving in this way makes both people unhappy, and can lead to things getting worse.

Look up the Lord's Prayer in the Bible. What does it say here about forgiving? God can only forgive us if we are prepared to forgive other people who have hurt us. Jesus told a story about a man who would not forgive. It is a picture of the teaching here. Read the story, and prepare the dramatised reading. Let the children divide into small groups and act out situations where forgiveness is needed, e.g. calling someone names, hitting each other, not letting someone join in a game, ganging up against someone. Choose two or three of these for performance.

Participants: Readers – Peter, Jesus, servant, fellow servant, king.
Actors – king, servant, fellow servant, other servants, guards.
Children to act in playlets.

Children to read prayers.
5 groups for choral speaking.

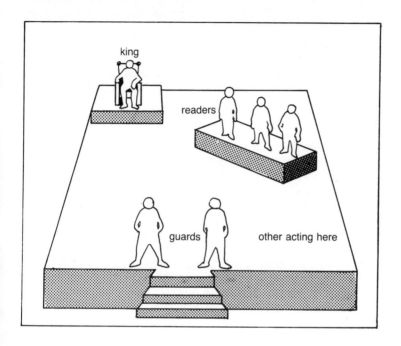

PRESENTATION

Hymn: 'Father, hear the prayer we offer' (Sing to God 121)

Prayer: 'The Lord's Prayer' (*If your school does not use this, have the words written large, or on the overhead projector so that everyone can join in.*)

Forgive us our trespasses, as we forgive those who trespass against us. What do you think that means? (*Wait for answers from the audience.*)

One of Jesus' friends wanted to know the answer to a question like that too. Listen.

(*The reading is taken from Matthew 18 verses 21 to 35. Start with the words 'Lord, if my brother. . . .' The actors should listen to the reading and do what the words suggest, miming only while the various voices are read by other children.*)

We have been thinking about forgiving. Sometimes it is not very easy to forgive. It is much easier to stay cross. Also it is not always easy to say sorry when we know that we need to be forgiven. We have made up some plays showing people either forgiving or not forgiving each other. See if you can work out which people are behaving as

Jesus would have wanted them to, and which are not.

(*Four or five little playlets can be performed here. These should have been worked out by the children previously, some showing children behaving in a loving way, others showing people not willing to forgive each other.*)

All through the Bible we can read of places where God's people realise they have done wrong things. In each case they come back to him and ask him to forgive them. Just as God forgave them when they were sorry so he will forgive us. Listen to some of the prayers of people in the Bible.

Choral speaking.
(*5 groups of children.*)

Group 1	There is no other God like you, O Lord.
Group 2	You forgive the sins of your people. You do not stay angry for ever,
Group 3	(*quietly*) but you take pleasure in showing us your constant love. You will be merciful to us once again.
Group 2	(*loudly, perhaps with a stamp of the foot*) You will trample our sins underfoot and send them to the bottom of the sea.
Group 3	You will show your constant love to your people.
Group 4	(*joyfully*) Praise the Lord my soul. All my being praise his name. Praise the Lord my soul and do not forget how kind he is.
Group 5	He forgives all my sins.
Group 1	The Lord is merciful and loving, slow to become angry and full of constant love. He does not keep on punishing.
Group 2	He is not angry for ever.
Group 1	He does not punish us as we deserve, or repay us for our sins and wrongs
Group 4	As high as the sky is above the earth, so great is his love for those who honour him.
Group 5	As far as the east is from the west, so far does he remove our sins from us.
Group 3	If we say that we have no sin, we deceive ourselves and there is no truth in us.
Group 4	But if we confess our sins to God, he will keep his promise and do what is right; he will forgive us our sins and purify us from all our wrongdoings.

(*Taken from Micah 7:18–20, Psalm 103:1–4; 8–13, 1 John 1:8–10.*)

Hymn: 'My Lord, my God' (Sing to God 105)

Prayers:
Three or four children could read their own prayers about forgiving and being forgiven.

FOLLOW UP

1 Discuss the importance of being prepared to say sorry to other people. This is the 'other side' of forgiveness; we have to be prepared to accept forgiveness. Discuss the saying 'it takes two to make a quarrel'. What do the children think this means? Can they write stories to illustrate it?

2 Look up other teaching about forgiveness in the Bible. Matthew 6:14, 15, Psalms 32, 51.

3 Read extracts from Lorna Doone explaining that it was lack of forgiveness that resulted in so much unhappiness. Encourage the children to write stories about rivalry between families/gangs and how they were resolved.

27 The lost son

AIM

To show God as a loving father who wants the best for us his children.

BIBLE BASE Luke: 15:11–25

Jesus was talking to a group of tax-collectors and other outcasts. Tax-collectors were despised by other Jews because they collected taxes for the Roman overlords and often demanded extortionate sums of money in order to line their own pockets. On the edge of the crowd stood some Pharisees, gazing critically at Jesus. Because they kept the law of God outwardly and added many rules and regulations to it they thought themselves vastly superior to these men. They could not understand why Jesus should want to talk to such 'sinners'.

To show how different from this God's attitude is, Jesus told three parables, the lost sheep, the lost coin, the lost son. All are found in Luke 15.

NB Pigs were considered unclean animals by the Jews and they would never keep pigs nor eat their meat. For this reason the idea of looking after pigs was particularly abhorrent to the farmer's son.

The parallel of a loving father must be treated very sensitively since there may well be some children in our classes who will not be familiar with the concept. Some children may not have received much real love and kindness and their understanding of 'love' will be confined to the sentimentality of 'pop' songs.

CLASS PREPARATION

Ask the children if they have ever run away from home, or at least wanted to.

Ask how they were received when they returned home or why they did not actually go. They could write a story about running away – either real or imaginary.

Read or tell the story of the boy who left home (Prodigal Son) in Luke 15:11–24 and explain simply that we are like the boy and God is like the father in the story.

Participants: *Acting* – non speaking – servants, farm hands, friends.
                      speaking   – son, father, narrator, 2 friends, farmer
Children with prayers.

PRESENTATION

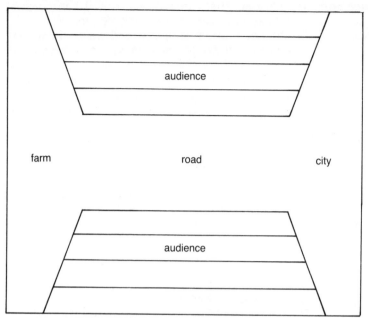

farm   road   city

*Let the children act this 'on the flat', with the audience in
two parts either side of the 'road' leading from the farm to
the town. On the farm, you will need several servants and
farm-hands, miming the various jobs to be done on a farm.
At the end the servants bring the items requested by the
father. They could continue miming throughout the action.
In the town, you will want a group of 'friends', dancing and
eating and drinking.
The son walks through the audience on his way to and
from the town.*

Hymn: 'You can't stop God from loving you' (Sing to God 19)

Narrator	Jesus told this story:– There was once a farmer who had two sons. He loved them both very much. One day his younger son came to him,
Younger Son	Father, I know that one day your money will be divided between my brother and me. I want my part of it now so that I can go away and have a good time. Will you give it to me?
Father	My boy, think carefully. Do you really want to go away and leave your home and family?
Younger Son	Yes. I'm fed up with being here on the farm all the time. There's nothing to do but work. I want to go and meet people and enjoy myself while I'm young.
Father	*(sadly)* Very well. If that's what you really want. I'll give you your share of my money.
Narrator	So the father got the money together and gave it to his son.
Father	Here you are, my boy. Use it well. Remember, I have

	nothing more to give you now.
Younger Son	Thanks Dad, that's marvellous. Now I can go away and do as I like, and no one can stop me.
Narrator	So the boy packed his things and went off. He went to the town and bought new clothes and everything he wanted. In the big city he soon made lots of friends, when they saw he had plenty of money. And he spent it freely. Every night he gave parties and bought drinks for his new friends. Everything seemed to be going his way. Then his money began to run out.
Younger Son	I'll ask my friends to lend me some money. I've done so much for them, they are bound to help me now.
1st Friend	Sorry, I haven't anything to spare. I'm just going out to buy myself a new coat.
2nd Friend	You've run out of money? Hard luck! I don't suppose I'll be seeing you around any more then.
Narrator	Not one of his friends would help him. He was left alone.
Younger Son	I must try to find a job so that I can buy food. Excuse me, sir, have you any work I can do?
Farmer	You can go and look after my pigs.
Younger Son	Look after pigs? Me? Oh no!
Farmer	Please yourself. That's all I have to offer.
Younger Son	(*hesitates*) We–ll. Oh all right, I *must* do something to get food.
Narrator	So he went to look after the pigs. But the farmer didn't give him anything to eat. Soon he was so hungry he wanted to eat the pigs' food. Then he began to think.
Younger Son	How stupid I am, sitting here looking after pigs, with nothing to eat. I'm dying of hunger, yet in my father's house everyone has plenty to eat. I must have been mad to leave home, . .I know what I'll do. I'll go home and tell my father that I was wrong. I'll say 'Father, I know I've done wrong against you and against God. I don't deserve to be your son but please will you take me back as one of your servants.'
Narrator	So he began the long walk home, ragged and dirty, and weak with hunger. As he limped up the road towards the house he saw the front door open and someone come running out.
Father	My son, how good to see you. I have been watching for you for so long.
Younger Son	Father, I have done wrong. I am not fit to be your son.
Father	Come quickly everyone. See what has happened. My son has come home. Bring out the best clothes and put them on him. Give him some new shoes, and put my ring on his finger. Kill the best calf and cook it. We'll have a feast, for my son, whom I thought was dead, is alive. He was lost and is found.

Narrator	Jesus said God is like that Father. When those who have done wrong come back to him and say they are sorry, God is glad and forgives them.

Prayer:

Now (*names of 2 children*) will lead our prayers.

Dear Heavenly Father, thank you for the story of the boy who ran away. Please help us to be sorry as he was when we do wrong. Amen.

Dear Lord God, we thank you that you are like that Father, always loving us and ready to welcome us when we come to you. Amen.

FOLLOW UP

1 Read or tell the other two parables in Luke 15, the lost sheep and the lost coin, and compare the three. How are they alike and how unalike?
2 Discuss the various ways of using money. How do they use their money now? Make some graphs.
3 Find out which animals are regarded as unclean or sacred in different countries and why.

28 Helping

AIM

To encourage the children to be ready to help anyone in need.

BIBLE BASE Luke 10:25–37

The lesson this story contains is that helping each other is important and that it is not who you are, or what you say that matters but what you do. The priest and the Levite were important respected people, and they thought they were doing right; but it was the Samaritan who proved himself to be a true neighbour, or friend.

The Levite. This may need explaining for the children. Levites were people who worked in the Temple. Though they were not priests, and could not offer sacrifices, they were still dedicated to God, and as such should have been ready to show kindness. Both the Levite and the priest represent the people who could have been expected to help the injured traveller but both failed.

The Samaritan was a member of a race despised by the Jews (though not by Jesus who broke the taboos by speaking to and teaching them, John 4:1–42). The reasons for this mutual dislike were historical. Originally the inhabitants of Samaria had been part of the Jewish race, but over the years they had intermarried with people of other tribes (something that God had told his people not to do), and so were no longer pure-bred Jews. As such they were no longer considered to be part of the 'covenant people'. Not unnaturally the Samaritans resented this attitude, and in turn hated the Jews.

The road from Jerusalem to Jericho was notorious for robbers. It was a mountainous road, providing many hiding places and escape routes for gangs of thieves. It is possible that 'injured' men were used as 'bait' to catch travellers who stopped to give help, but this did not excuse those who callously passed by.

CLASS PREPARATION

This could be introduced from an example of classroom helpfulness. Discuss with the children the need for helping each other in various ways at school and at home. Let them write about ways they help and ways in which other people have helped them.

Children could think of people they know who need help; handicapped, lonely and old people in particular. Remind the children of any efforts the school makes to help less fortunate people.

Talk to the children about first aid. This is a specialised kind of help. The Red Cross Handbook provides useful information. Children should know how to react in an emergency, and how to give elementary first aid for cuts, bruises and shock. Encourage them to talk and write about when they received or gave first aid. What happens in school when someone hurts themselves?

Put the question, 'Would you help someone you didn't like?' Jesus told a story to show how we should behave towards people in need, whoever they are. (Explain that Jews and Samaritans did not like each other.)

Having set the scene, describe the long and dangerous route from Jerusalem to Jericho, a road beset by robbers until recent years. Help the children to imagine the feelings of someone setting out. He would want to reach his destination as quickly as possible. No doubt he would travel with others if this was at all possible. The road descended about 1000 metres in less than fifteen miles. Gorges and rocks provided good hiding places for robbers. Children could draw and paint scenery for use in the assembly.

Participants: 6 children talking about first aid.

Acting – Priest, Levite, Samaritan, wounded man, robbers.

Other children will have painted 'scenery' for the play.

PRESENTATION

Useful Props: Strips of old sheet for bandages, plastic bottle and portable first aid kit, pictures of the Jericho road.

Hymn: 'When I needed a neighbour' (Someone's Singing Lord 35)

Introduction

We have been talking and writing this week about first aid. This is our first aid box. We use it when we go on school visits.

Three children I needed first aid when. . . . .

Three children I gave first aid when . . . .

Staging: *Try having the 'audience' in two sections with a central aisle or 'road' and let the action be along this instead of at the front as is usual.*

Jesus told a story about a man who needed first aid. We are going to act it for you.

Priest   I work for God as a priest in the Temple at Jerusalem. Now I must hurry home to Jericho.

Levite   I am a Levite. I work in the Temple too. I must get home to Jericho before dark.

Samaritan   I am a Samaritan. I have been visiting Jerusalem. Now I must get home to Jericho.

(*These three could all speak their lines from one end of the room. The 'robbers' could have been previously placed about halfway along the 'road' amongst the audience. The man who is attacked could start from Jerusalem as soon as the other three have finished speaking.*

About halfway along, the robbers spring out and attack him. Slow motion 'fighting' is very effective and means that no one need actually touch anyone else. He lies down as if dead, and the robbers disappear into the audience again.)

Priest   (*walking along the road*) Who is that? He must have been attacked by robbers. They might still be hiding somewhere. . . I had better get away fast or they might catch me.

Levite   What's that over there?. . .I'll have a look. Oh, poor man. . . .He must have been attacked by robbers. Well, there's nothing I can do for him. I must hurry home in case they attack me too. .

Samaritan   Who's that? I'll look and see. Oh the poor man, he must have been attacked by robbers. . .But he's still breathing. . . I must see what I can do.

(He gives the man a drink and bandages his wounds, then lifts him up gently and supports him along the rest of the road.)

Come, I'll take you to a hotel down the road. I know the owner will look after you well.

Prayers: Thank you, Lord, for people who help us when we hurt ourselves. Thank you for the Red Cross and the St John's Ambulance Brigade. Thank you for the men and women who take sick and injured people to hosptial in ambulances.

Help us to remeber what to do when someone cuts themselves or gets a bruise. Amen.

Show us how we can help when someone needs a neighbour – may we never be too busy to help them. Amen.

There are other ways of helping people too. These children are going to mime/have written/drawn some. . .

Hymn: 'Look out for loneliness' (Someone's Singing Lord 36)

FOLLOW UP

1 Make sure all possibilities from the preparation section have been fully explored. Use the opportunity provided by the raising of the subject of helping to discuss and improve general class helpfulness, and perhaps extend this by helping in other ways, e.g. visiting an old people's home, knitting squares for a blanket, etc.
2 Look up stories of people helping each other in the Bible, e.g.
Exodus 4:1–18 – Aaron and Moses
Exodus 18:13–26 – Judges for the people.
Acts 11:27–30 – Church members helping each other
3 Also look up stories in the gospels of Jesus helping and healing people, e.g.
Luke 7:1–10 – Roman officer's servant
Mark 3:1–5 – Man with paralysed hand

Matthew 8:28–34 – Men with demons
Matthew 9:1–7 – Paralysed man
Matthew 15:21–28 – Canaanite woman's daughter

4 Other topics which could usefully be studied include First Aid, Travel in New Testament times and today, the Red Cross and St John's Ambulance Brigade and the emergency services, particularly the Ambulance Service. You might be able to arrange for a member of the Ambulance Service to visit school and talk about his work.

29 Come to the party

AIM

To encourage the children to make time for learning about God.

BIBLE BASE Luke 14:15–24

Jesus was having a meal at the home of a leading Pharisee (Luke 14:1). The Pharisees kept the law of Moses very strictly and Jesus had already angered them by healing a sick man on the Sabbath day. One of the guests remarked, 'How happy are those who will sit down at the feast in the Kingdom of God.' It was to him that Jesus spoke this parable. He showed that it is a joyous, happy thing to follow God's teaching and serve him.

It was an Eastern custom to send out servants to remind guests that the feast was ready.

CLASS PREPARATION

Ask the children if they have ever had a party invitation that they refused. Did they have a real reason for not coming or did they make an excuse? Discuss the difference between a reason and an excuse.

Jesus told a story about people who made excuses. Read or tell the story. Let them make a montage, i.e. a large number of pictures mounted together on one large sheet of paper or board, to illustrate a party. Divide the children into groups; one group to draw or paint pictures of flowers which could be used to decorate a room for a party, another group to draw or paint other decorations such as balloons, banners and streamers, and a third group various party foods. Encourage them to work in bold, clear colours. If preferred, some of the children could cut out pictures of flowers from seed catalogues and food from magazines, and arrange them to form a picture. Stick the completed pictures on to your large sheet of paper with blu-tack so that they can be removed and stuck on again during the assembly. Overlap the individual pictures to give a 'oneness' to the finished montage.

When the pictures have been placed in the best positions, draw lightly round the outline of each picture on the background, and number each one so that when the children stick on their pictures during assembly, they will know where to place them. It's important that the numbers should be placed so that the last ones can still be seen when the others have been placed.

Participants: 2 readers, narrator

Acting – rich man, 3 guests

Children with pictures for montage

PRESENTATION

Hymn: 'Choose you this day' (Sing to God 116)
'Follow, follow' (Sing to God 119)

Leader Jesus said that following his way and doing what he says is the happy way of living. But many people are so busy with their own affairs that they don't bother to think about God's way.

1st Reader Have you ever been too busy to visit your grandmother, or to go and see a friend who is ill, to help your mother with the washing up or to play with your little sister or brother?

2nd Reader Perhaps you were too busy watching television, or playing football with your friends, or sorting your stamp collection.

Leader Jesus told a story about people who were too busy.

(*Narrator sits in centre of stage area. On one side sit three children representing the guests who made excuses. On the other side is a chair for the rich man and the board for the montage.*)

Narrator There was once a rich man who planned to have a big party.

(*Rich man enters and sits on the empty chair.*)

Narrator When everything was ready the rich man sent his servant to tell the invited guests that it was time for the party to begin. Then every single one of them began to make excuses.

(*The three guests stand in turn to make their excuses and then walk out.*)

1st Guest I'm sorry I can't come. I've just bought a field and I have to go and look at it.

2nd Guest I've just bought some cows and I have to go and try them out to see if they are all right. Please excuse me.

3rd Guest I've just got married, so I can't come.

Narrator When the servants came back and told their master that no one was coming he was very angry.

Rich Man Very well then, go out into the streets of the town and bring in the poor people, the sick, the blind and those who can't walk.

Narrator All these people were very glad to be invited to the party and they all came. The house was full and they all had a wonderful time, but not one of the man's friends was there.

Leader That man's friends were too busy to have time for him. In the same way some people are too busy to have time for God, but God will always welcome those who will come to him.

Hymn: 'I cannot come' (Sound of Living Waters 115)

Prayer: Heavenly Father, we thank you that you want us all to come to you and be your friends. Please help us not to be so busy with our own things that we have no time for you. Amen.

FOLLOW UP

1 If the children have learned the song 'Choose you this day', they could look up the reference to it in Joshua 24:14,15 and read or listen to some of the stories of Joshua's exploits in the book of Joshua.

2 Jesus told other stories about what it would be like in his Kingdom. Read these:

    Luke 13:18,19 – Parable of the mustard seed
    Luke 12:35–48 – Parable of the servants

See other outlines in this section for more stories Jesus told.

SECTION 4: SPECIAL OCCASIONS

30 Crossing the Jordan

An assembly for the beginning of a new school year.

AIM

To show that God gives us opportunities to start again.

BIBLE BASE Joshua 3,4

The story of the Israelites' entry into the Promised Land is one of a real new beginning. After 40 years of wandering in the desert, they were finally to have a home; the chance to settle down and give up their nomadic existence. Their past failures, mistakes and wanderings were all behind them. The fact that God made the River Jordan dry up so that they could cross was a sign of his protection and care for them. The stones were to be a permanent reminder to them that they had been given this land by their God.

CLASS PREPARATION

As the children return to school after the summer holidays many of them will be making a new beginning in a new class with a new teacher. You could introduce the assembly preparation by asking what is different in this class from the one they were in last term. Are there things they like better or less?

Mention 'new year resolutions'. Could you draw up a list of 'new school year resolutions' for your class and all try to keep them? Can they suggest some for their teacher?

Talk about memory joggers. How do the children remember things; do they write notes, tie knots, etc? The stones in the story were memory joggers.

Let the children write about important days in their own lives. Have they been told about events in their parents' and grandparents' lives? If so, why were these events remembered?

Participants: Children to read 'resolutions'.
Acting – Narrator, Joshua, priests, messenger, people of Israel, river Jordan, twelve stone gatherers.
Musicians.
Children to read prayers.

PRESENTATION

Hymn: 'God who made the earth' (Sing to God 20)

It has been quite some time since we have all been together in this hall for an assembly, in fact some people here have not been to one like this before. The beginning of a new year in a new class or school can be quite exciting – a real new beginning in our lives. Each new class gives us a chance to work harder, to make new friends, to leave behind some of the things we did last year, to learn all sorts of new things.

In our class we have been making 'new year resolutions'. Listen to some of them. (*Three or four children read theirs.*) I wonder if these will last any longer than the usual kind.

Some of the people who were here with us last term have gone on to make a really important new beginning; they have started at their secondary schools. We have been thinking about some people who made a real new start, almost a new life. Watch.

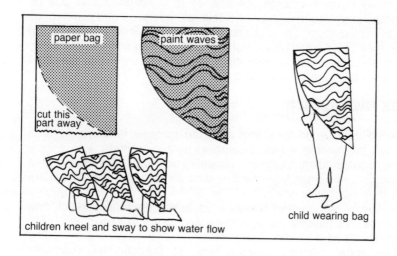

paper bag

paint waves

cut this part away

children kneel and sway to show water flow

child wearing bag

Props: Several large pieces of paper or paper carrier bags, painted blue and cut as shown in the diagram to be used by the children representing the river Jordan. Twelve large stones. Box representing the Ark.

Characters: Priests, Joshua, messenger, twelve stone gatherers, people. Also musicians, playing percussion and recorders or guitars for the accompanying music.

(*Start with the river in the first position, swaying gently to suggest waves. Let the musicians make up water music for this part. As the Narrator starts to speak the music will need to fade out. While he is speaking, the people all come to settle down on one side of the river, acting as if they have come a long way, sitting down and pretending to cook food, or falling asleep for example.)*

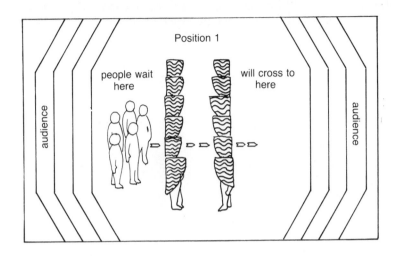

Position 1

people wait here

will cross to here

audience

audience

Narrator   The people of Israel had been wandering in the desert for a very long time. God had promised them a new land to live in, but they had not believed that he could give it to them, and so they had disobeyed him. As a result they had been going round and round in the wilderness intead of settling into their new homes.

The river Jordan was the boundary to this land; once they had crossed it they could begin a new life; no more wandering, they could build homes and plant crops. But the river was in flood when they reached it.

(Here the watery music could get louder again and the children acting the river could move more violently.)

Narrator   The people did not know what to do. God told Joshua that he would make a way for them to get across and he was to tell the people to get ready.

(Joshua stands up, walks around as if thinking, then beckons the messenger who goes round all the people, 'talking' to them. As he does so, the people stand up and gather up all their belongings, and begin to form a line, starting at the river's edge. Music at this point could be 'busy' music, lots of instruments played very fast. At the head of the line should be the priests carrying the Covenant box.

Narrator   Joshua told twelve men to pick up a stone each and carry it to the other side with them.

(Stone carriers pick up heavy stones, and join on the end of the line.)

Narrator   Joshua signalled to the Priests to step into the water. . . .

(As they do so the music should stop suddenly, then perhaps a drum roll or cymbal as the water begins to move.)

Narrator   . . . and as they did so the water piled up on either side, forming a dry pathway for the people to walk across. The priests stood where they were till all the people had crossed.

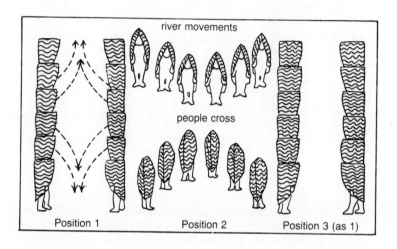

(Water moves as indicated in the diagram (Position 2). People show surprise and fear, they then begin to cross. Marching music might be appropriate here. As the stone bearers reach the other side they put their stones down in a pile. You could have them make quite a ceremony of this, with a drum beat for each stone put down, and clapping from the people.)

Narrator   As the men carrying the stones reached the other side, they put their stones down in a pile, forming a memorial mound, to remind people in years to come how God had made it possible for them to start a new life in the Promised Land. When all the people were safely over, the priests crossed, and as they stepped out, the waters rushed back together again.

(Priests cross, to marching music again; the waters move as indicated in the diagram (Position 3) and the watery music could start again.)

Narrator   The people knelt to thank God for getting them safely across the river, then danced with joy that they were in the Promised land at last.

(Music all quiet as the people all kneel, then when they get up, you *could have lively music for them to dance to. The dance could finish by them all kneeling again.)*

Hymns: Choose You This Day (Sing to God 116)
O Jesus, I have promised (Sing to God 114)

At the beginning of a new school year God gives us a chance to make a fresh start.

We can decide to improve our work and be better behaved, but most important of all we can make up our minds to try to live the sort of lives God wants us to live.

Prayers: *(The children may be encouraged to write their own prayers.)*

Heavenly Father, thank you that you gave your chosen people a chance to turn from their wickedness and make a new start in a new land. Thank you that you have given us a chance to make a fresh start in school at the beginning of this new year. Please help us to make good use of all the opportunities we have in school to learn together, so that all our lives may be pleasing to you. Amen.

FOLLOW UP

1 Look at the wanderings in the wilderness in greater detail. Exodus.
2 Look at the story of Rahab and the spies, stressing the new beginning in Rahab's life after the fall of Jericho. Joshua 2, 6:25.
3 Discover how the Israelites conquered Canaan. Joshua 5–12.
4 Make a frieze of events from the plagues in Egypt to the crossing of the Jordan.
5 Let the children write 'eyewitness' accounts of the crossing of the Jordan.
6 Encourage the children to compare the life of the Israelites before and after crossing.
7 Think about other ways of commemorating important events. Visit local memorials.
8 Look up other 'water miracles'. Exodus 14:10–30 – crossing the Red Sea. Mark 6:48–51 – Jesus walks on the water

This assembly could be followed by Outline 5 where the Israelites begin to take possession of their land.

31 Harvest

AIM

To encourage children to appreciate the goodness of God's creation.

BIBLE BASE Genesis 1

The first chapter in the Bible sets out to tell the story of the creation of the world by God. It sets the world in relation to the one who formed it. It is important to remember that there are many different *theories* about how the world was formed; there is no authoritative scientific account. Evolution and creation are not necessarily contradictory. It would be best not to try to explain here as you will only risk confusing the children. If they are told that Genesis tells us it happened, but does not go into detail about how, they will be quite satisfied.

CLASS PREPARATION

During Autumn, children often bring in berries and fruits, and you could start your discussion of harvest and creation from there. Your school will probably be making a collection of items for a harvest festival in any case, but, if not, why not have a class collection to put on display during the assembly? You will also want to collect food items or craftwork from various countries for the presentation.

Talk about the many different edible plants that are grown in this country. How are they harvested and when? What things that we eat come from other countries? Do the children know anything about how they grow and are harvested? You could collect labels, make maps, etc.

Ask the children if they have ever thought about how it all began. Where did the very first plant come from? Read Genesis 1. They may have all sorts of comments about it, so you will want to have time to discuss it. In preparing the dance, it is probably best to let all the children together work through the various 'events' before trying to put anything together. This way they will each feel, through having mimed it, the whole of the creation story.

Participants: 29 dancers.
18 children to bring gifts.

PRESENTATION

Hymn: 'When God made creation' (Sing to God 21).

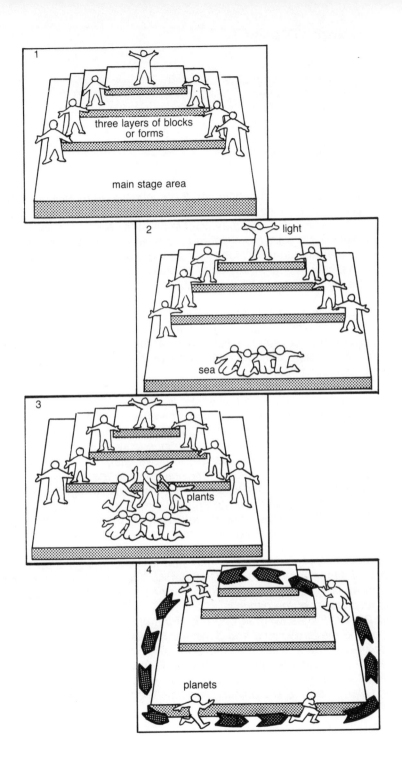

Dance based on Genesis 1.

Cast: Light: 1 child
Water: 6 children plus 4 children.
Plants: 5 children
Planets: 2 children
Fishes: 3 children
Birds: 3 children
Animals: 5 children
Man
Woman

(*These numbers are the minimum. It is suggested that the whole class take part in the dance, so more can be added. If the bringing up of gifts is to be included, you may want to enlist the help of another class, especially if you want the children to appear in national costume.*)

The teacher should read *Genesis 1* as the children dance; make sure there is plenty of time for the actions. Music such as 'Venus' from 'The Planets' by Holst could be played quietly throughout.

vs. 1–2. *Children move around wildly (they could come on stage doing so) and swirl around chaotically, flinging arms and legs about, with no pattern to their movement (Diagram 1). At the end of verse 2 they sink to the floor, where they will need to be for their next part, and lie quite still in crumpled heaps.*

v. 3. *'Let there be light.' One child springs up, on to highest block and stands with arms stretched upwards, lifting face as if to the sun.*

vs. 6–7. *All the other children kneel up and sway as if they were water (Diagram 2). Those 6 who are to be the 'dome' move to their places and take up position. They should continue to sway gently throughout. NB Leave room behind for 'planets' to move later.*

vs. 8–10. *The children kneeling all sink down to the ground and stay still except the other four water children, who move together to form the sea, and sway gently (Diagram 3).*

vs. 11–12. *The 'plants' grow up into various shapes, and hold their positions (Diagram 3). They may move gently as if blown by the wind from time to time, or droop and 'die' and then grow up again.*

vs. 14–19. *The planets get up and start to move in large slow circles around all the other children (Diagram 4). They need not necessarily all move in the same 'orbit', or at the same speed. They continue to do so for the rest of the dance.*

vs. 20–23. *Fishes swim in and out of the children who are being the sea, and the birds fly up and down the blocks supporting the 'dome'.*

vs. 24–25. *The animals move amongst the plants. Try to have a good variety of movement, and also choose distinctive animals.*

vs. 26–31. *The girl and boy get up and wander amongst the animals and plants, looking and pointing and touching things, seeming to enjoy what they see.*

Prayer:

Our Father God, we thank you for all the things you made when you created this world; for beautiful birds and pretty flowers, for fruit of all kinds for us to enjoy. Thank you too that you have given us the changing seasons. Thank you specially now for this time of harvest, when we can remember to thank you for all that the earth gives us. When we look at the things we have collected here, may we remember that they are proof of your love for us. Amen.

Leader	We are going to bring some of the things that we need to survive, and also things to enjoy; things God provided when he made the world. They come from many different countries.
English children	We bring corn and bread, the staff of life.
Asian children	We bring rice; the 'daily bread' of people in many countries.
Indian children	From India we bring tea, and the things of beauty made by our skilled craftsmen.
West Indian children	Coconuts, bananas and sugar all grow in the West Indies.
Australian children	Wool and meat are some of Australia's exports.
New Zealand children	From New Zealand we get butter and cheese.
Danish children	From Denmark we get bacon and more butter.
Dutch children	Holland produces many special cheeses.
Spanish children	From Spain we get oranges and chestnuts.

(*This list can be added to or adapted as time and space permit*).

Hymn: 'We plough the fields and scatter' (Sing to God 23)

FOLLOW UP

1 Work on imports and exports can be done, using a large map to stick on labels from various products from all over the world.

2 Choose crops from two or three different countries, preferably with very different growing and harvesting methods, for study in depth. The children can draw pictures to illustrate the various stages each one goes through.

3 The children could draw large pictures to make a frieze of the creation story.

4 Jesus told many stories using the familiar farming life of his time. Look up some of these to find out something about farming in Bible times. How is it different from now? Matt. 13:3–8, 24–32; 18:12–13; 21:28–31.

5 Look up other portions of the Bible which are concerned with creation: Psalm 93, 104, 148; Job 36:27 – 41:34

See also outline 11 for a similar theme.

32 Christmas

AIM

To remind the children of the true meaning of Christmas.

BIBLE BASE Luke 2:1–20

The facts of the Christmas story will be familiar to most Junior age children though they are still quite likely to have areas of confusion.

It is assumed that the school will have some sort of Christmas performance; this assembly could be used as part of this or as a school assembly in the normal way.

The miracle of the angel telling the shepherds of the birth, was a sign from God that this was a very special child – God's own son – and it is his birth we celebrate today.

CLASS PREPARATION

The children will be well into preparing for Christmas by the time you want to prepare an assembly; the shops will have had decorations and tinsel up for months, and your problem will not be how to get the children thinking about Christmas, but how to stop them long enough to get any work done!

You could introduce your assembly theme by asking them to write about what Christmas means to them, and listening to and comparing the results. Presents and food will probably be well to the fore, but some children will mention the Christmas story. Explain that the reason for all the celebration is because a very special baby was born: God's Son. The festivity reminds us, or should, of what a very important event that was for all of mankind all through the years.

Remind the children of the facts of the story. This could be retold with the room lit by candles, (well out of reach). Ask them to write Christmas poems and carols following this, and compare these with the writing they did before.

Participants: Groups of children to mime Christmas preparation. Actors: Mary, Joseph, star, shepherds, angels. (optional actors – animals, villagers) Musicians. Children to read poems and prayers.

PRESENTATION

Carol: 'The Virgin Mary' (Sing to God 58)

In our class we are busy getting ready for Christmas; and I expect it's the same in yours. See if you can guess what these children are doing. (*Several groups of children come on in turn and mime such activities as making paper chains, stirring the Christmas pudding, wrapping up presents, making cards, decorating the tree, lighting candles, etc.*)

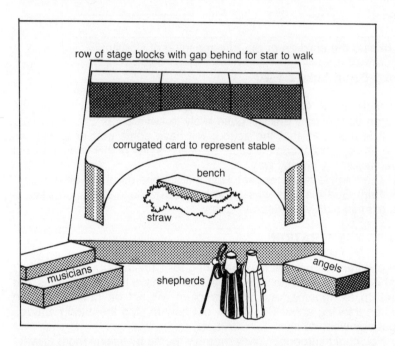

row of stage blocks with gap behind for star to walk

corrugated card to represent stable

bench

straw

musicians

shepherds

angels

All these things are very exciting, aren't they, and we spend a lot of time trying to get everything just right for Christmas. But sometimes amongst all the fuss and excitement we forget what it is all about. We'd like to remind you now, who we are getting everything ready for.
Carol and mime.
(*The children should have learnt the carol and some sort of musical accompaniment should be arranged using the skills of the children involved – percussion, at least, but guitar and recorders if these are available as well.*)

Characters: Mary with baby, star, Joseph, shepherds, angels, musicians. The carol is 'The Calypso Carol' (Sing to God 60)
Verse 1 (*Mary and Joseph come on and gently lay the baby in the straw. You could include animals, with cardboard masks here if you want to involve more children; in which case the animals should be led on by 'villagers' who then retire before Mary and Joseph appear.*)
Verse 2 (*The star could be hidden by stage blocks so that all that is seen is a moving star, which comes to rest behind the baby [see diagram]. Shepherds should have been lying asleep during the first verse and now get up ready to look at the angels in verse three.*)

Verse 3 (*Angel choir sings to the shepherds then moves to the stable, followed by the shepherds.*)

Verse 4 (*As many of the musicians as can, move towards the 'stable' and kneel in front of the baby during this verse.*)

Now let's all sing a carol. 'Silent Night' (Sing to God 59)

The important thing about Christmas is that it was the time when Jesus was born. It is his birthday we are celebrating. Listen to these poems. (*If you have a suitable poem written by one of the children, which makes this point clearly, then use this and omit all speech here. Several children could read their poems.*)

Prayer: Let us pray.

Dear Lord Jesus, we thank you that you came to earth at Christmas time many years ago and were born a baby, so that you could grow up to teach us all about God. Thank you that we have this happy time to remember you by. Please help us to make you the most important part of our Christmas this year. Thank you for loving us so much that you were prepared to come and be born in a dirty, smelly old stable. Please help us to love you too. Amen.

(*Again if you have suitable children's prayers use these instead*).

Carol: 'Once in Royal David's city' (Sing to God 50)

FOLLOW UP

1 There will probably be very little time for follow up work, but your

children might like to write out the Christmas story and illustrate it to take home to read to their families on Christmas day.

2 Ask the children where they were born. What would it be like to be born in a stable? What would be missing that they had as babies? Could they compare their early life with that of Jesus? See Matthew 2 for more of Jesus' early life.

3 Let the children imagine they are one of the people involved in Jesus' birth, a shepherd, the innkeeper, or Joseph for example. Let them write the story from this point of view.

4 If you have time, make a crib or a frieze of the Christmas story for the classroom.

33 Palm Sunday~Jesus borrows a donkey

AIM

To tell the facts about Palm Sunday, emphasising people's response to Jesus.

BIBLE BASE Luke 19:28–40

Jesus went into Jerusalem on a donkey because it had been prophesied that this was what the Messiah would do. Zechariah 9:9. A donkey was a sign of peace – kings normally rode a horse. He was proclaiming in an unmistakable way who he was. This is one reason why the Pharisees were so cross. The ordinary people were acclaiming him as much by using the words they did. Psalm 118:26.

CLASS PREPARATION

Most schools tend to discourage children from lending their personal possessions to each other. But it does happen. Discuss with the children occasions when they have needed to borrow something. Let them imagine the following incident:–

Mum, Dad and the family are at home one afternoon watching television. They are very excited. The Queen is visiting their town. Dad said that the centre of town where the Queen was to open a new hospital would be packed. So they were going to have a good view of the event on television. They settled down in front of their set to watch and wait. Dad was just beginning to doze when there was a knock at the front door. Mum went to see who it was. She came rushing back shouting, 'Dad, come at once. There's a man at the door. He says the Queen's car has broken down outside. Could she borrow our car to drive into town?'. . .

Jesus borrowed several things while here on earth, including a stable for his birthplace, a donkey, an upper room and a tomb.

Donkeys have always been valuable beasts of burden in eastern lands. They are strong and sure footed on rough roads and trackways. The unknown owners of the donkey were committed to serving Jesus in any way they could. He really was their Lord.

Participants: Four children with writing
Seven children for choral speaking
Actors – Mother, Sarah, Mark, Father, Matthew, John.

Children to contribute to the prayer
Rest of children for the crowd on the road.

PRESENTATION

Hymn: 'Jesus was the Son of God' (Come and Sing 31)

Have you ever thought what you would do if the Queen came to our town? Or even our school? We do have a lot of visitors, but if the Queen came what a lot of preparations we would have to make. If she came to our town, people would be getting ready for weeks. These children have written about what they would do if they heard that the Queen was coming to visit us.
(*Three or four children*)
Well, she would be really pleased, I am sure. But suppose she came and no one was expecting her. She would just see our town as it is every day. Perhaps she would like it that way.

When Jesus came to our world as a baby, only a few people were expecting him. But when he began to do his wonderful work, healing people who were sick, crowds came to see him and listen to his stories. Sad to say, there were some people who were jealous and wanted to kill him.

Near the end of his life here on earth, Jesus was going to Jerusalem. Long before this a man of God called Zechariah had written:–

Choral speech:
Group of 6:   Rejoice, rejoice, people of Zion!
Shout for joy, you people of Jerusalem!
Look, your King is coming to you.
He comes triumphant and victorious,
Solo: but humble and riding on a donkey,
on a colt, the foal of a donkey.

(Zechariah 9:9)

He was writing about what Jesus was going to do. Jesus was about to do what Zechariah had described. Most people did not know who Jesus really was. But those who loved him would do anything for him, as we shall hear in our story.

Mother   I hear Jesus is coming to our village.
Sarah   Can we see him, mother?
Mother   Yes, of course, Sarah, we have a lot to thank Jesus for.
Mark   What do you mean?
Mother   Before we met Jesus we were a sad family. But he made us happy. Didn't he, father?
Father   Yes, that's right. I said to Jesus, 'If ever you need my help just let me know, Lord'.

Just then, two men were coming.

Matthew	This is the village, John.
John	Yes, Matthew, and look, there is the house. And the young donkey tied up outside – just as Jesus said.
Matthew	Remember, we are to say, 'The Lord has need of it'.

(*disciples mime untying 'donkey'*).

Mother	What are you doing with our donkey?
Matthew	The Lord has need of it.
Mother	(*to father*) He says the Lord would like to borrow our donkey.
Father	That means Jesus wants it. Yes, I am glad I can help him.
Mother	Yes, you can borrow our donkey. We are so pleased to help him.

So the disciples took the donkey and Jesus rode on it to Jerusalem.
(*Crowd cheers as Jesus rides by.*)

Prayers:
Just as we thought about the man who helped Jesus by lending him his donkey, we are going to think about how we can help people we know. I want you to say 'Please show us how we can help them', when I pause.
(*Let your class add names to these categories; they will be able to suggest people who especially need prayer.*)
Dear Lord Jesus, we pray today for
  sick and lonely people
  our mothers and fathers
  our brothers and sisters
  our friends at school
  our teachers
  our school caretaker and cleaners
  our school cooks and dinner ladies
The Lord's Prayer

Hymn: 'Praise King Jesus' (Come and Sing 29)

FOLLOW UP

1 Follow through the events leading up to the death of Jesus.
2 Make a large picture of the entry into Jerusalem using individual pictures of the people in the crowd, Jesus and the disciples, to join together into one large scene.
3 Make a frieze of the events of the last week of Jesus' life.
4 Look up another 'donkey' story in the Bible (Numbers 22:22–35). Make a book of these two rewritten in the children's own words.
5 The idea of sharing was very important in the early church. Jesus and his followers did not regard personal possessions as being very important. Look up Acts 4:32; Matthew 6:19–21, 25–34. Can the children think why today we put so much stress on having? Is it a

good thing?

The following two assemblies continue the story of the last week of Jesus' life.

34 Easter: darkness to light

AIM

To present the facts of Good Friday and Easter.

BIBLE BASE John 18:28–19:30. Philippians 2:6–11

The passage in the Gospel of John presents the facts of Jesus' trial by Pilate and his death. This is a straightforward account, which is why it is used here in preference to those in the other gospels. There are parts of the trial of Jesus, (his appearance before the High Priest) which have been left out from the assembly outline. These could be included in class work.

Crucifixion was a Roman way of executing criminals and it was a particularly cruel and lingering death. The beating before it was also very painful as the whip would have had little pieces of lead on the thongs.

The several trials which Jesus was subjected to were because there really was no charge against him; the Jews thought he was guilty of blasphemy, ie. of claiming to be God, but this was not a crime by Roman law so the charge of claiming to be king was trumped up.

The resurrection is important because it is proof that he was God, that his claim was not blasphemy but the truth.

The passage in Philippians is included because it is a concise summary of what Christians believe to be the significance of Jesus' death. It is a form of creed, which you may wish to omit.

CLASS PREPARATION

You will need to go into the story of Jesus' death and resurrection with your class before they start making the picture for use in assembly. You could read portions from the Bible at storytime, for a week or so, or retell it in your own words. Alternatively use one of the filmstrips recommended in the appendix. Children will probably be very sensitive to the suffering and injustice in the story and you may have to spend quite some time talking about this. Let them write about aspects of the story.

After talking about Jesus' death, ask the children what their feelings about such a death would have been. Was there a reason for it or was it just a waste? Explain that at first his followers saw his death as the end of everything:– a tragic mistake; but when he came alive again they saw that there was a purpose to it.

Read the passage in Philippians with your class. What does the writer see as the reason behind Jesus' death? Does this make sense to them?

Talk about the difference Jesus' resurrection made to his disciples; it was like a new day dawning; life had begun again in a new way. Can the children express these two feelings; that of utter despair, then of hope renewed, in dance? Let them experiment, then work out a dance for use in the assembly.

Participants: Children for introductory miming
Readers: Pilate, Jesus, Jewish leaders, Temple guards, crowd, narrator, soldiers.
Dancers: minimum of 6 children.
Choir (optional)
Choral speaking: minimum of 8 children.

PRESENTATION

Hymn: 'There is a green hill' (Sing to God 77)

(*After the hymn two or three children could enter eating Easter eggs, and talking about what they are going to do during the school holidays*).
Leader: Is that what Easter means to you; chocolate eggs and a holiday from school? It means a lot more than that to Christians. It is a time that is just as important as Christmas, but in a different way. At Easter we remember that Jesus died . . . listen while we read you some of the story.

Reading

Dramatised reading of John 18:28 – 19:16.
(*This can be read almost word for word from the Bible. If the children can memorise their parts so much the better. Leave out anything that prevents the action from flowing freely, for example such words, as 'they answered, he said'.*)

You will need speaking parts as follows: Pilate, Jewish leaders, Jesus, Temple guards, crowd, narrator, soldiers.

Let the children work out in advance what actions they want to make at the various parts of the narrative; they may need quite long pauses in the speaking to fit in all they want to do.

Hymn: Now we are going to sing a hymn that tells us some of the rest of the story; 'What do I see' (Sing to God 85).

Reading: 'After Jesus was handed over to be crucified, it was not long until it was all over. Listen. (*It is suggested that the rest of the story John 19:17–30 is read either by a teacher or by four or five very competent readers. It is not possible to act this part convincingly, but if it is read with feeling the children will identify with what is happening*).

Pause at the end of the reading for a few seconds.

All this happened on the first Good Friday. But strange as it may seem that was not the end of the story. Three days later, on the first Easter Day, Jesus came alive again. We have tried to show the difference this made to his friends in a dance. Watch.

The dance should be performed while a choir or the whole school is singing hymn 90 in Sing to God, 'Low in the grave he lay'.

Dance
Verse one
Dancers kneel with heads bowed, as if crying, around an imaginary or real 'body'. At the first chorus all leap to their feet, flinging their hands up into the air, and throwing heads back. They turn to face outwards, and walk around in a circle.

Verse two
At the beginning of the verse the dancers form into two rows of 'soldiers' with spears. They mime standing at ease then to attention. At third line they mime rolling a big stone into position – either as a group or as individuals. At the beginning of the chorus the soldiers fall to the ground and cover their faces as if afraid. Then all point and look upwards. They could then run away.

Verse three
Dancers return to starting positions. Slowly raise their heads looking surprised, then joyful, lifting hands above heads. Stand up at line three, and join hands, swinging them slightly and walking round in a circle. At beginning of chorus drop hands and jump round to face outwards, throwing hands into the air. Join hands above heads then walk round taking large strides and keeping hands joined above heads, looking pleased and confident. At line three, drop hands, then making an upwards movement, clap hands for line four. For the last line the children could jump four times clapping their hands above their heads, and end standing with hands above heads and heads thrown back.

You see, the fact that Jesus had come alive again frightened the soldiers but made his friends very happy. Listen to what St. Paul said about his death some years later.

Choral reading: Philippians 2:6–11.
Two groups of children and two solos.

Group 1	Jesus is the Son of God.
Group 2	He was willing to become man.
Group 1	He was willing to be obedient to God and die on a cross.
Group 2	(*loudly*) For this reason, God raised him to the highest place above,
Group 1	and gave him the name that is greater than any other name.
All	And so in honour of the name of Jesus,
Solos	all beings in heaven,

Group 1   on earth
Group 2   and in the world below,
All   will fall on their knees.
            And all will openly proclaim that Jesus Christ is Lord
            to the glory of God the Father.

(NB If you have many children from other faiths, you may well feel the need to omit this reading, as it is quite explicit in its statement of who Jesus is.)

Hymn: 'The angel rolled the stone away' (Sing to God 88)

FOLLOW UP

1 Talk about the meaning of Jesus' death if you have not already done so.
2 Look up resurrection stories. Luke 24:13–52; John 20:1 – 21:24.
3 The children could write Easter poems and hymns, with music.
4 Compare how the disciples must have felt on the Friday evening with how they felt on the Sunday evening when they had seen Jesus alive again. Let them write about this (John 20:19–23).

35 Seeing is believing - or is it?

AIM

To show that because the resurrection really happened, we can believe in Jesus today.

BIBLE BASE Luke 24:13–44. John 20:24–29.

John was the beloved disciple who was describing the events he had seen with his own eyes. Luke was a later convert, a Greek doctor travelling with St. Paul. Although he had never seen Jesus, he took great pains to collect evidence from eye-witnesses before writing his Gospel.

CLASS PREPARATION

Make sure your class are familiar with the story of the death of Jesus and the events of Easter morning. Use resources from the appendix to help here. Are there things the children can think of that have happened to them that have seemed impossible? Or are there times they could write about when their feelings have changed from despair to joy, or some other great change?

The question of whether we have to see before we can believe could be discussed by the class. What things can they think of that they believe in without being able to see? Are there any times they can think of when what their eyes have told them is wrong? (Have any of them seen themselves in distorted mirrors for example?) Could the children write stories in which things are not what they seem? Prepare for the drama by asking the children to write about how Thomas and the other disciples might have felt. What would they have thought? Use these ideas to encourage them in the rehearsals for the play.

Participants: Eleven disciples, Jesus, Teacher, two children, rest of class.

PRESENTATION

Start by reminding children how the disciples must have felt on Good Friday evening – bewildered, upset and sad, hopeless. They had completely forgotten what Jesus had told them many times. Read Matthew

16:21, stressing the last few words. Jesus had known that he was going to die and he had told them that on the third day he would come alive again. Count off the days on fingers, Friday was the first day, then Saturday, now we're going to see what happened on the Sunday evening. The disciples have just seen Jesus and are talking about what has happened.

Scene 1

Ten disciples in the upper room. Let them 'ad lib' dialogue along the lines of 'how wonderful it was to see Jesus again' 'I remember now he said he would come alive again' *etc. Someone should say* 'pity Thomas wasn't here'.

Enter Thomas. All crowd round him talking excitedly. Thomas looks confused, asks them to calm down and tell him one at a time, which they do eventually. He thinks they've all gone mad and gets angry when they try to convince him. Blurts out that he'll only believe when he can see and touch Jesus, and runs off.

Break off the drama here, Say, 'We'll see in a little while what happened next. But first we're going to think about what Thomas said. He said he couldn't believe unless he saw. He thought seeing was believing. Just because we haven't seen something with our eyes does that mean it can't be true?'

Watch this: (*one sketch is suggested here, your class might like to make up their own, to substitute or add*).

Teacher	Now, class, where did you go for your holidays?
Child 1	Please, Miss, I went to Clacton.
Teacher	Yes a very nice place. I went there when I was a little girl.
Child 2	Please, Miss, I went to Lyons in France.
Teacher	Nonsense, child, there's no such place. I would have been there if there was.

The teacher did not believe there was a place called Lyons because she had never been there. She would only believe in things she had seen for herself. But there are many things that we believe in even though we have not seen them ourselves, like different countries, volcanoes, whales, and so on. There are other things that we believe in even though they cannot be seen. We know that our parents love us even though we cannot see the thing called love. We believe in the wind because we feel it on our faces, and see it moving the trees, but we have never seen 'wind'. Thomas did not believe what he could not see for himself. But he was to find out how wrong he was.

Scene 2

All the disciples are together, including Thomas. Jesus must be concealed behind a curtain or screen. Disciples talking about the events of the week before when they had seen Jesus. Thomas is still very depressed. One of them says 'Wouldn't it be wonderful if Jesus was here with us now!' *Jesus steps into view. Most of the disciples have their backs to him – including Thomas, and if they can hide his entry from the audience this would be even better. Someone sees him and points 'Look he's here.' Conversation between Jesus and Thomas. Jesus must be very gentle as he says,* 'Well come on then Thomas, you wanted to see my hands. Come and touch them if you can't believe your eyes!' *Thomas falls down and worships Jesus.*

Jesus said that people who could believe in him without actually seeing him would be happy or blessed. And that includes us too. We can read the events of his life and resurrection as written down in the Bible by disciples who actually saw and touched him. And we can read how he changed their lives. We can read about people down the ages who have believed in Jesus. And we can meet and talk to Christians today, who believe without ever having seen Jesus. In fact they would probably say that instead of 'seeing is believing' it's the other way round, 'Believing is seeing'.

Prayer:
Let's end with a prayer.

Thank you, Father that you never force people to believe in your son. We pray that you will show us the truth about Jesus as we think seriously about what we've heard from the Bible today.   Amen.

Hymn: 'Low in the grave' (Sing to God 90)

FOLLOW UP

1 Read the resurrection accounts from all four Gospels. Matthew 28, Mark 16, Luke 24, John 20, 21.
2 Make lists of the people who actually saw Jesus and where they saw him. See also Acts 1:1–11 and 1 Corinthians 15:3–9.
3 What parting instructions and promises did Jesus give his followers before he went back to heaven? Acts 1:4–5, 7–8; Luke 24:47–48; Matthew 28:19–20.
4 Discuss variations in the Gospel accounts of the empty tomb. Matthew 28:1–15, Mark 16:1–12, and Luke 24:1–11. Discuss reporting events from different angles, eg. sporting events. What facts do all accounts clearly agree on?
5 Rewrite one of the resurrection accounts as if you were the eye-witness.
6 Draw the story in comic strip form.
7 Make a list of words describing the feelings of either Mary Magdalene or John at the foot of the cross and then when they met Jesus on Easter morning. Make them into a poem.

36 Mothers Day

AIM

To make the children appreciate the care a mother gives to her children.

BIBLE BASE Exodus 2:1–10

This is a well-known story, the background to which appears in the previous chapter. By killing all the Israelite boys, the Pharaoh hoped to reduce the Israelites' potential power; see Exodus 1:9–10. Moses, however, was protected in a very special way; he had a job to do.

CLASS PREPARATION

Mothering Sunday presents an opportunity to remind children of the love and care given to them by their mothers. Discuss with them what their mothers do for them during a typical day. Suggest they ask their mothers what they like doing best and least and how much time they spend ironing, cooking, cleaning and making beds. The children may well be surprised to discover how hard their mothers work while they are at school. Many will have mothers who have a job to do outside the home as well. Preparation for Mothering Sunday provides the children with an opportunity to say 'thank you' to their mothers by making a card and perhaps a simple gift.

Encourage the children to think what they do, or should do, for their mothers. This will vary according to the age and maturity of the children, but we should help them to respond positively to their mothers' care.

There will be children who have no mother or whose mothers do not show the love and care we have spoken about in the preparation. You will need to be sensitive to them.

The Bible teaches that mothers are to be honoured and obeyed (see Exodus 20:12 and Deuteronomy 21:18–20). Challenge the children as to whether they always obey their mothers! Remind them that Jesus obeyed his mother and father (Luke 2:51).

Invite mothers to the assembly.

Participants: Girls with dolls or children to mime and sing.
Actors: King, father, mother, Princess, servant(s), Miriam.
Children with prayers.

PRESENTATION

Hymn: 'Let us thank the heavenly Father' (Infant Praise 35)
Today we are thinking about our mothers.
(*Use either of the following introductions*)
A. These girls have brought their dolls. They are going to show us some of the things a mother does for her tiny baby.
Examples:– washing, dressing, feeding, putting to bed.
What a lot a mother has to do for her baby every day.
B. We have been thinking about our mothers and the things they do for us. Here is a song called 'A Mother's work is never done'. (*One child mimes the actions for each verse. The tune is 'Here we go round the mulberry bush'.*)

1 This is the way she cooks my meals, cooks my meals, cooks my meals. This is the way she cooks my meals, every day of the year.
2 washes the dishes
3 makes the beds
4 cleans the house
5 mends my clothes
   We have also been thinking how we try to help our mothers.
6 This is the way I make my bed . . .
7 tidy my toys
8 wash the clothes
9 clean my room
   every day of the year.

Now we are going to have a story about a baby boy who was in great danger. Our story begins in the palace of the King of Egypt.

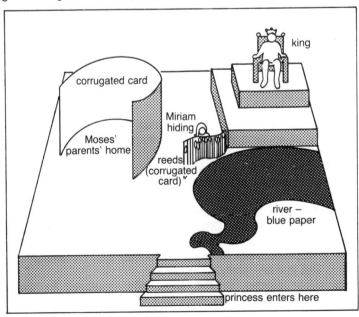

37 Whitsun

AIM

To teach of the coming of the Holy Spirit at Pentecost.

BIBLE BASE Acts 2:1–42

Jesus told his disciples about the Holy Spirit and who he is (John 14). He is the third person of the Trinity and he guides (John 14:16), comforts (Acts 9:31), strengthens (Acts 1:8), empowers (1 Corinthians 12), discerns (John 16:13), makes sense of God's word (John 16:13).

When Jesus went up to heaven, he told his disciples to wait for the Holy Spirit to 'come on them', giving them the courage and power they needed to carry out his command to go and make disciples (see Matthew 28:16–20). This passage (i.e. Acts 2) gives the fulfilling of this promise, and the consequent change in the behaviour of these once timid believers. Summarise Peter's speech by saying that Peter told the people about Jesus. The content of Peter's 'sermon' seems rather complicated to us as it draws heavily on Old Testament material, but we should remember that he was speaking to Jews, and using their Scripture to prove to them that Jesus was the promised Messiah.

CLASS PREPARATION

Discuss with the children the need that we all have for someone to help us from time to time. Often we can do things with help that would be quite impossible alone. Let them give examples, and write stories about helping. Jesus' friends were like this too. After he had gone back to heaven, they were scared and did not know what to do. But he had promised them another friend to help them and one day a very strange thing happened to them. The Holy Spirit came to them. The Holy Spirit is that part of God who makes God real to us and gives us the power to follow God's ways. Read the story in Acts 2 with the children. Prepare a dance drama to represent the events of the story. The children who perform the dance would need to practise moving in time to the telling of the story.

Participants: Children to demonstrate in introductory activities.
Reader(s)
Musicians
Dancers – Twelve disciples
Children to read prayers

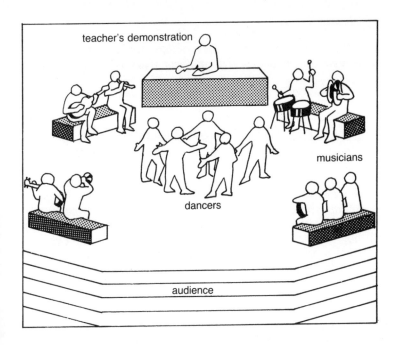

Diagram labels: teacher's demonstration, musicians, dancers, audience

PRESENTATION

We have been thinking about things that need help in order to work properly.

Firstly a sponge. What do we use a sponge for? This sponge when it is in contact with water becomes full of water and so it is useful for cleaning. (*Demonstrate on dirty object*).

This sponge, however, is not in contact with water and is hard and dry. It cannot be used to clean (*demonstrate*) and is therefore useless.

If I pour water onto the sponge, its usefulness returns because it has come in contact with water. So a sponge needs water to make it useful.

Here is an overhead projector, but it is not plugged into the socket. Is it useful like this? What is the source of power which makes it useful? Without its source of power the overhead projector is useless.

Hymn: 'Spirit of God' (Sing to God 102)

Now here is a true story about a group of people who, like the sponge, and the overhead projector, became useless for a time, until the source of their strength and power returned.

Jesus had promised his friends that when he went back to heaven he would send them a helper, the Holy Spirit, to give them the power and the courage they would need to tell the world about him and to carry on his work. We have made up a dance to show you the difference it made to them when the Holy Spirit came to them.

Reader: Acts 2:1–4.

Dance: Twelve disciples, musicians.

Sound effects on percussion, recorders, guitars, for wind and fire, also for talking in various languages. The musicians could use their voices here too.

1 Disciples are sitting in a circle, heads bowed and hands hanging down.

2 Wind music, soft at first, then getting louder. Disciples start to sway from side to side as if being blown by the wind. As it gets stronger they rise to their feet, still swaying. Wind suddenly stops and disciples stand quite still.

3 Fire music. Disciples point to each other's heads, put hands up to their own. Looks of fear, then wonder and joy. They could begin to dance and jump about and perhaps join hands. It is important to get across that they are thrilled about what is happening to them. Up to this point they have all been facing towards the centre of the circle.

4 When talking music begins they all turn to face outwards, and move hands, arms and faces as if talking.

5 The dance could end by the disciples reaching out their hands to the musicians as if asking them to join them. The musicians leave their instruments and join the circle. All then join hands and raise their arms to heaven, then kneel down as if praying.

The disciples were able to tell other people about Jesus because the Holy Spirit helped them. Some of the people listening came to join them and so the Christian Church began to grow.

Prayer:

Like the disciples, we need Jesus' help in everything we do, so let us ask him to give us, through his Holy Spirit, the power to live useful lives for him.

Dear Lord Jesus, Thank you for the gift of your Holy Spirit to the first disciples. Often we are useless, like dry sponges, because we do not ask for your help and we try to live without you. Please give us the Holy Spirit to help us understand your word and to give us power and strength to tell others about you. We ask this for your glory's sake. Amen.

Children could be encouraged to write prayers.

Hymn: 'When God the Holy Spirit' (Sing to God 103)

FOLLOW UP

1 Look in detail at Peter's speech in Acts 2.
2 Look at further manifestations of the Spirit's power, in healing (Acts 3, 4), in freeing the prisoners (Acts 5).
3 Look at the lives of eminent Christians who display God's power in most adverse circumstances, eg. Corrie Ten Boom, Brother Andrew.
4 Look at symbols of the Holy Spirit and develop these in art work

– dove, flame.
5 Develop the theme through dance, focusing on vertical to horizontal movements (showing power coming down – then out to others).

See outline 20 for a follow-up to this outline.

You will need to explain to the children that the book of Proverbs, parts of which are used in the assembly, is a book in the Bible giving advice as to how to live a happy and successful life. It is thought to have been written, at least in part, by King Solomon, the king who asked God for the gift of wisdom. Proverbs are 'wise sayings'. The children might know some 'proverbs', which they can think about. What does 'the early bird catches the worm' really mean, for example? Perhaps they could paint illustrations of some of these proverbs.

Participants: Sixteen children for choral speaking
                      Minimum four musicians
                      Four children to read

PRESENTATION

(*The passages for speaking by a teacher are for guidance only; you may well want to change the actual words to suit your particular situation; for example if teachers are leaving too*).

'What we call the beginning is often the end. And to make an end is to make a beginning. The end is where we start from.' These words were written by a writer called T. S. Eliot.

Today as we draw near the end of our school year it is true to say that we are all making an end and that end is also a beginning. All of us have nearly finished our time in one class, and after the holidays will be making a start in a new class, at the beginning of the new school year. But for some of us this is a very special end; the end of our time in the Junior school, and the start we will make is also very special. It will be the start in a new school. It is one more step for these people to make in the journey of life.

Hymn: 'One More Step' ('Come and Praise' Publ. BBC)

These children are going to recite a passage from the Bible which talks about the different times there are in life.

Choral speaking:
                      Solo voices 1 and 2
                      Group 1 – six voices
                      Group 2 – four voices
                      Group 3 – four voices
                      Musicians – suggest drum, tambourine, cymbal,
                                  recorder.

(*Drum beat or short haunting recorder melody*)

Solo voice 1	Everything that happens in this world happens at the time God chooses.
Solo voice 2	He sets the time for birth
Group 2	and the time for death (*low and monotone*)
Group 1	the time for planting and the time for pulling up
All	the time for killing (*strongly*)
Group 2	and the time for healing (*gently, but not whispered*)

156

All	the time for tearing down and the time for building. He sets the time for sorrow (*softly*) and the time for joy (*louder, tambourine*)
Solo voice 1	The time for mourning
All	and the time for dancing (*tambourine*)
Group 3	the time for kissing and the time for not kissing. He sets the time for finding
Group 1	and the time for losing the time for saving and the time for throwing away
All	the time for tearing
Group 2	and the time for mending
(*Pause*)	
Solo voice 1	The time for silence (*slightly echoing stage whisper*)
(*Pause*)	
Group 2	and the time for talk
(*over the next three lines build up a crescendo*)	
Groups 2 & 3	He sets the time for love and the time for hate. The time for war (*cymbal clash*) (*Pause until clash has completely died away.*)
Solo voice 2	And the time for peace.

Suggested grouping for choral speech

Group 1

Group 2

Group 3

Group 4

Prayer: Almighty God we give you thanks for the world and all your good gifts; for the sky above us and the earth beneath our feet; for our homes, our families, our school and our friends. Thank you for the term that is coming to its end and for all the fun that we have had.

Thank you for all the opportunities we have had to learn. Forgive us for time wasted and unkind words and actions. Help us to use the knowledge we have gained not only for ourselves but also for others. Amen.

(*Use this in place of the prayer*)
We have had a lot of different experiences during the last year. Think about all the things that have happened to you . . . all the things you have learnt . . . all the skills you have acquired . . . Think about how you can use these past things to build on in the future.

Hymn: 'Saviour teach me' (Hymns of Faith 446)

Teacher: For everything there is a time. For some of the people here today their time in this school is nearly over. They will soon be leaving us to go on to their secondary schools, or a new home, or a new job. To all these people we have to say a special thank you. Thank you for any service you have given in the school, as monitors, or helpers, or as team captains. Thank you for the sports, the plays, the singing and the music in which you have taken part. We hope you will take happy memories of your time here to your new schools. Listen now to some advice from the Bible.
Four children: 'Trust in the Lord with all your heart. Never rely on what you think you know. Remember the Lord in everything you do and he will show you the right way. Never let yourself think that you are wiser than you are. Always remember what you have learnt. Your education is your life – guard it well.'

Hymn: 'The journey of life' (Someone's Singing Lord 28)

FOLLOW UP

None is included as it is not imagined you will have time for any!

RESOURCES SECTION

BOOKS FOR USE IN ASSEMBLY

General

Stories for the Junior Assembly	Blandford Press
More stories for the Junior Assembly	,,
The Reluctant Mole	Scripture Union
Ignatius goes Fishing	Scripture Union
Seal Songs and other stories	Scripture Union

Prayer Books

365 Children's Prayers	Lion Publishing
When you pray with 7-10s	Denholm House Press

Bible Stories

Ladybird Bible Books, Jenny Robertson	Ladybird/Scripture Union
Listen – Themes from the Bible	Collins
Praise – Songs and Poems from the Bible	Collins

Hymn Books

Come and Sing	Scripture Union
Come and Sing some More	Scripture Union
Sing To God	Scripture Union
Come and Praise	BBC
Praise God Together	Scripture Union
Someone's Singing Lord	Black
Merrily to Bethlehem	Black
Carol Gaily Carol	Black
Sound of Living Waters	Hodder & Stoughton
Faith, Folk & Clarity	Stainer and Bell
Hymns of Faith	Scripture Union
BBC Hymn Book for Junior Schools	BBC

BOOKS FOR USE IN CLASS AND FOLLOW UP

Stories for children to read
Ladybird/SU Bible Books	Ladybird/Scripture Union
Ladybird Religious Topics Series	Ladybird
Little Lions	Lion Publishing
What the Bible Tells us Series	Bible Societies

Children's reference books
Little Lions — Lion Publishing
Ladybird Religious Topics Series 522, 606A, 612, 640.
Life in Bible Times — Scripture Union

Teacher's Reference Books
Good News Bible
Lion Handbook to the Bible — Lion Publishing
Lion Encyclopedia of the Bible — Lion Publishing
Look into the Bible — Scripture Union

FILMSTRIPS

Scripture Union Soundstrips include
    Luke Street Series
    Discussion Starters Series (some parables among others)
Tear Fund Sound strips on world resources, division of wealth, etc. for children.